فتاوى النساء

FATWAS OF
Muslim Women

IBN TAYMIYYAH

TRANSLATED BY
SAYED GAD

Qadeem Press Edition

Translation of the Qur'ān It should be perfectly clear that the Qur'ān is only authentic in its original language, Arabic. Since perfect translation of the Qur'ān is impossible, we have used the translation of the meaning of the Qur'ān throughout the book, as the result is only a crude meaning of the Arabic text.

Qur'ānic verses appear in speech marks proceeded by a reference to the Surah and verse number. Sayings (Hadith) of Prophet Muhammad (saw) appear in inverted commas along with reference to the Hadith Book and its Reporter.

Table of contents

- Translator's note...............21
  Purification...............23
- Altered water because of its being in a place
  for a long time...............23
- Men and women having Ghusl (purificatory bath)
  from the same container...............23
  Copper utensils inlayed with silver...............24
- Circumcision of women...............25
- Wiping over the head cover...............26
- Touching women...............26
- Touching the Holy Quran...............28
- Carrying the Holy Quran...............28
- Reading the Qur'an during puerperium
(Nifas)...............29

- Prayer...............30
- Making up missed prayers...............30
- Is making up missed prayer better Than performing
  optional prayer ?...............31
- Woman's ornament...............31
- Concealing women's private parts from men and
  Women...............34
- Showing the face, the hands, and thefeet before
  Strangers...............36
- Does a woman have to cover her hands in prayer?......38
- The uncovering of a woman's hair during prayer........41
- A woman praying with the surface of her foot
  uncovered...............41

- Sewing silk for men and women and getting
  paid for it...42
- Women's wearing kaffiehs....................................43
- The criteria of imitating the other sex.....................44
- Women's wearing turbans.....................................48
- Is a Christian woman to be buried among Muslims? ..48

- Zakah...49
- Zakah of Jewelry..49
- Zakah on a woman's dowry....................................50
- Can the grandmother be a legitimate recipient
  of Zakah if in debt?..52

- Fasting...53
- Is a pregnant woman, who is in no pain, allowed
  not to fast for the safety of her baby?.....................53
- What is a fasting Muslim allowed to do? What
  would break his fasting and what would not?.................53
- A man who could not fast or pray right before
  his death...55
- Refraining from going to extremes in
  worshipping Allah...55
- A woman going on a pilgrimage without an
  unmarriageable kin..57
- Can a woman go on a pilgrimage on behalf
  of another?...58
- Can a woman who has already performed the
  pilgrimage go on a pilgrimage on behalf of a
  dead person and be paid for it?.............................58
- Circumambulation of the Sacred House made by

a menstruating woman..59
- Attending 'Arafah by a menstruating woman.............63
- A weak woman who spends the night in Muzdalifah...63
- Circumambulation made by one who is ritually
  impure due to menstruation, seminal
  discharge or   due to minor impurity i.e. not
  making ablution...64
- Forbidding a menstruating woman to observe
  Fasting in Ramadan...74
- Forbidding a menstruating woman to perform

- Prayer...74
  Recitation of the Holy Qur'an by a menstruating
  Woman...78
- Menstruation and I`tikaf (Seclusion in a Mosque
  for worship)..79
- The prayer of a menstruating woman....................105
- From Endowment to Marriage............................113
- Is it permissible to build a second floor over
  a Mihrab (altar)?..113
- Assigning a will or an endowment for one's
  Neighbors...113
- The unmarried reciter..114
- Is it permissible to privilege some of the children
  with a portion of the estate to the exclusion of
  others? Is it permissible to give to relatives
  from the estate?...114
- A woman dwelling next door to a group of men
  and a mn dwelling next door to a group
  or women...115

- Assigning an endowment for the needy relatives
  of the deceased...116
- Assigning the revenue of endowments for
  shrouding the poor deceased..................................117
- Gift and gratuity Charity and present.....................117
- The Undefined Gift..118
- A Woman Giving a Book to Her Husband
  as a Gift..121
- Privileging one of her children from a different
  husband with a charity...121
- The charity of a grandmother................................122
- The distribution of the estate...............................123
- A father seizing the possession of his married
  daughter after her death......................................123
- Returning in a gift...124
- A divorcee returning in her gift............................125
- A man returning in his gift which he made to
  his wife after her death.......................................125
- Remitting a husband from the dower at the
  wife's death..125
- A gift given to the wife and children......................126
- A father returning in his gift to his bad son............127

- BEQUESTS...127
- A bequest or an acknowledgment of a debt?............128
- Making bequests of unequal shares to
  one's children..129
- A postponed oath...129
- Annulment of a bequest.......................................129
- Can a nephew be an heir?.....................................130

- A bequest to a husband and a paternal uncle and a grandmother...........131
- A bequest of Hajj...........131
- Benefit for the deceased...........132
- The guardian of the orphan girl...........133

- IHERITANCE...........134
- The share of the widow...........134
- The share of the husband from the inheritance of his deceased wife...........134
- How to distribute the estate?...........135
- The sisters and the daughters...........135
- Paternal and maternal brothers and sisters...........136
- A husband, mother and maternal sister...........136
- A daughter, maternal brother and a male cousin...........137
- A husband, father, mother, son and daughter...........138
- The distribution of the estate between the husband and the nephew...........138
- The daughters of one's brother...........140
- A divorced-thrice-widow...........140
- Divorce before consummation of marriage...........141
- A husband who divorces his wife before his death in way to disinherit her...........142

- MARRIAGE...........145
- Proposing to marry a woman already engaged to another person...........145
- A woman proposed to during her 'Iddah (waiting period)...........146
- Muhallil (a man who married a woman then

divorces her so that she may return to her
previous husband who irrevocably divorced her).....146
- The second proposal.................................147
- Private meeting of a man with a woman................148
- The divorced thrice..................................148
- The proxy of a dhimmi in marriage of a Muslim.....150
- Marriage in illness...............................152
- A woman marrying with a guardian other
  than her father..................................152
- A lying woman who changes her name and the
  name of her father...............................153
- Obligation of the virgin major woman..............157
- Marrying a woman to her relative against her will....164
- Guardianship of a stranger........................165

- WOMEN FORBIDDEN IN MARRIAGE..............166
- The Exchange Marriage [*Shighar*]......................166
- Combining a woman and her maternal aunt
  in marriage......................................167
- Taking in marriage the paternal aunt of
  a man along   with his niece..........................167
- Marrying the mother of one's wife with whom
  marriage is not consummated..........................169
- 12 moths without menstruation!...........................170
- Menstruation twice only.....................................170
- A virgin woman who is divorced thrice..................171
- The marriage of a woman whose guardian is
  a *fasiq* [oft-sinner].................................171
- Conditions of marriage fulfilling the conditions
  of marriage......................................172

- Physical defects versus marriage.............................174
- Can leprosy cause the annulment of marriage?........174
- The *Mustahadah* [a woman suffering from
  continuous vaginal bleeding].................................175
- A woman found to be virgin..................................177

- ANAL SEX WITH WIVES.......................................177
- Is anal sex with one's wife is lawful?....................177
- *Nushuz* [disobedience of the wife] A woman who
   fasts during the day and prays during the night
   and refuses her husband's invitation to the bed.......178
- Divorce and analogous cases..................................179
- Khul' [demand of divorce made by the wife
   in return for a compensation given to
   the husband]..179
- Chula' in the Qur'an and Sunnah...........................180
- The forced divorce..180
- Accusing the wife of adultery................................181
- The Khul' of a woman who has no guardian...........183
- Cancellation of absolution.....................................184
- Divorce after the absolution of the dower..............184
- Revocable divorce of a deceived husband..............185
- A rule in khul'..186
- Is a Khul' counted in the three divorce pronoun
   cements?...186

- Zhihar...189
- What is the meaning of a husband's saying
   to his wife...189
- "You are just like my mother or sister"?

Is divorce effected if a husband demanded
to consummate marriagewith his wife on
a certain day but she was not ready on it?...............189
- Is it permissible for a man to reconcile with his
  wife even after he said to her: You are just like
  my mother as far as marriage is concerned?...........190
- When a man says that his wife is just like his
  mother during her absence, is she prohibited
  for him as a wife?...190
- When a man says to his divorced wife: If I
  resumed marriage with you, you will be just
  like my mother, what should he do?....................192

- Divorce..193
- Is a drunkard's divorce effected?.........................193
- Is divorce effeted when a man who lost his
  consciousness uttered it?....................................194
  If an angry man said: "she is divorced", but
  he did not mention his wife, is such divorce
  effected?...195
- Is divorce effected when a man is coerced
  to do it?..195
- If a man is coerced to divorce his wife and he
  did, but afterdivorce she got married to another
  man, is this marriage valid?................................196
- A man promised his wife to divorce her, but he
  had the intention to resume marriage with her
  and conclude a new marriage contract with
  another dowry, is this valid?...............................197
- Is it permissible for a man to divorce his wife

just because his mother hates her?.........................197
- When a mother wants to 'separate between'
  her daughter and her husband, is the
  daughter a sinner if she disobeyed her
  mother in this regard?.........................198
- Is divorce effected if the husband intends
  to divorce his wife before witnesses but
  he did not utter it?.........................199
- When a man thrice divorces his wife
  unintentionally and he means just once,
  is it effected?.........................200
- A man is indebted to his wife and he wanted
  to divorce her if he did not pay his debt. If
  she acquitted him from such debt, is divorce
  effected?.........................200
- Is it permissible for a man to re-marry his
  ex-wife whom he divorced thrice before
  consummating marriage with her?.........................201
- A woman is divorced thrice before consummating
  marriage and when she gets married
  again, she is also divorced thrice from thesecond
  husband before the consummation of marriage
  as well.Is it legal for her·to return to the
  first husband?.........................201
- Does a woman become prohibited for her
  husband if he said: All that I own is prohibited
  for me?.........................202
- When a woman says to her husband: "Divorce
  me" and he replied:"You are prohibited for me",
  is she prohibited in this case?.........................203

- Is it permissible to authorize the new wife to
  divorce the old one? Is divorce effected?.................203
- When a man's authorized agent thrice divorces
  his (the man's) wife, is it permissible for the
  husband to return to his wife?.............................205
- Is divorce effected when a man is forgetful
  or when he uttered wrong words?..........................206
- A man said to his wife: You are divorced if
  I see so-and-so at your house. Is divorce
  effected if he saw her in another place?.................207
- If the wife got out of the house without her
  husband'spermission while he swore an oath
  that she should not do so, is divorce effected?..........207
- A man accused his wife of stealing a sum of
  money and said to her: If you did not bring this
  money, you are divorced. Is divorce effected?..........208
- When the husband says to his wife: "you are
  divorced if you give birth to a female baby", and
  he revoked his threat. The woman gave birth
  to a female baby. Is divorce effected?....................208
- During a quarrel with his wife, the husband
  said: if you say "divorce me", I will do, but
  she kept silent. What is the legal ruling
  on this matter?..209
- If a wife enters a house forgetfully while
  her husband swears an oath of divorce that if
  she entered such house, she will be divorced,is
  divorce effected?...210
- Thrice divorce If a man swore an oath of
  thrice divorce not to enter his brother's house,

but later he was obliged to enter it, is
divorce effected? 211

- A man swore an oath of thrice divorce that he
  will leave the place where he lives. Later, he
  wanted to return. Is this permissible?.....................211
- An angry man swore an oath of thrice divorce
  that his pregnant wife should not enter her
  aunt's house. After giving birth, she entered
  this house. Is divorce effected?................................212
- Before his travel, a husband swore an oath of
  divorce that his wife should not get out of the
  house during his absence, but out of necessity
  ,she went out. Is divorce effected?..........................212
- When a pregnant woman refuses to have
  intercourse with her husband and he swore an
  oath of divorce that he will not have intercourse
  with her after giving birth. What is the legal
  judgementif he had intercourse with her after
  giving birth?..213
- When a man swears an oath of divorce not to
  have intercourse with his wife for six months,
  what should he do after the expiryof this period?......215
- Pending Divorce...215
- When a man swears an oath of divorce but he
  left it pending, is it effected?...................................215
- When a man says to his wife: "You are thrice
  divorced" and he has the intention to make it
  pending, is divorce effected?....................................216
- Suraij Question...217
- Is the Suraij Question true?.......................................217

- Is it permissible to make a marriage contract
  in which divorce is stipulated?....................217
- Lineage...218
- If a wife gave birth to a baby after six months
  of pregnancy,does this baby belong to
  her husband?..218
- Does the baby belong to the first husband if the
  wifemarried another man after her waiting
  period is over?...219
- A man divorced his wife but a Mufti delivered
  him a fatwa that divorce is not effected.
  The man had intercourse withhis wife and
  she gave birth to a child. Was the child born
  out of adultery?...221
- The child belongs to the conjugal bed....................222
- Invalid marriage contracts...............................223
- When a woman gives birth to a baby just two
  months after the marriage contract although
  the husband had not consummated marriage
  with her, is such marriage valid?........................224
- `Iddah (The Waiting Period)..............................226
- Is a woman's claim that she no longer
  menstruates accepted and she gets married
  according to it?...226
- When a judge abrogates a woman's marriage
  and her husband wants to return to her,
  is she entitled to a waiting period?.....................227
- A woman was divorced after giving birth to
  six children.After divorce, she did not
  menstruate for six months. Is it legal for

- her to marry another man after this period?............228
- When a suckling woman has a medicine so that she may menstruate and she has already menstruated thrice, does her waiting period come to an end?.................................229
- A sick man divorces his wife but later denied that he had done so. Days later he died. Is the wife entitled to a death or divorce waiting period?.....230
- Is a woman entitled to spend a death waiting period again if she did not spend it in her house?......231
- Is it permissible to engage a woman who spent just forty days out of the waiting period of her late husband?..............................231
- If a wife intended to perform pilgrimage with her husband, but he died before travel, is it permissible for her to perform pilgrimage?............232
- Suckling the baby..............................233
- When two sisters suckle the daughters of each other, is it prohibited for these daughters to
- marry their cousins?..............................233
- Two men were suckled by the same woman, then one of them got married and he had a girl. Is it permissible for the other man to marry this girl?..............................234
- When a girl is suckled with her cousin, is it permissible for him to marry her sister?.................235
- Is it permissible for the son of a suckling woman to marry the daughter of the girl who was suckled by his mother?..............................236
- A man married two wives and a baby was

suckled by one of them. This man had
a daughter born by the second wife. Now, is it
permissible for the suckled person to marry
this daughter? If they have already got married,
is it permissible for the judge to separate
between them?..236

- If a man was not suckled by the mother of
a girl neither was she suckled by his mother,
but their younger brothers and sisters
exchanged suckling from both mothers, is it
prohibited for this man to marry this girl?................237

- When one of two sisters is suckled with a boy,
is it permissible for him to marry
the second sister?...239

- When a boy is suckled with a girl, is it
permissible for his brother to marry her sister?.........239

- When a girl is suckled by her aunt, is it
permissible for the aunt's grandson to marry
 this girl?..240

- When a mother denied that she suckled a girl
married by her son, is it permissible to separate
between them?...241

- After a man got married and had many children,
he was told that his wife was suckled by his
mother. What is the legal judgment on
this matter..242

- If a man was suckled by a woman when he was
a baby and this woman has daughters younger
than him, is it permissible for him to marry
 any of them?...243

- Is it permissible for a man to marry a girl
  who was suckled with his brother?....................244
- A man used his wife's milk in washing his
  eyes and anothersuckled milk from his wife.
  Do their wives become prohibited?....................245
- A boy was suckled by a woman, and ten years
  later, she gave birth to a girl, is it permissible
  for him to marry this girl?....................246
- When a boy is suckled by a girl's mother and
  later this boy died, is it permissible for his
  brother to marry this girl?....................247
- A boy was suckled by the wife of his uncle
  when he was more than two years old, is it
  permissible for him to marry her daughter?....................247
- When a woman keeps her breast away from
  a baby once he starts suckling, is it permissible
  for him, once he is old, to marry this
  woman's daughter?....................248

- Alimony....................248
- A man divorced his wife thrice and he has a girl
  who is still suckled,is he entitled to pay alimony....................248
- When a woman needs money, does she take it
  from her husband or from her dowry?....................249
- When a woman disobeys her husband, is he still
  entitled to support her with money and clothes?....................250
- When a man leaves his wife for a whole year
  and does not support her with money, is it
  permissible for her to marry another man
  to support her?....................250

- After a man had married a woman, he left her for a whole year and traveled to his country. He did not send her money, is it permissible for the wife's father to abrogate the marriage?....................252
- When a wife travels with her father without her husband's permission,what is the legal ruling concerning them?.....................252
- A wife's family asked the husband to provide her with the clothes sufficient for a year and they have already obtained them. Then they demanded for money and said that they will support her. Is this act permissible?........................253
- When a man is imprisoned because he did not settle his wife's financial support and provide her with the necessary clothes, is it permissible for her to demand for support during his imprisonment?.....................255
- If a wife was of no avail to her husband for two years because of her illness, does she deserve financial support?....................256
- When a man divorces his wife while she is pregnant ,but later she was aborted , does she deserve alimony?.....................256
- Is the husband entitled to pay the waiting period alimony to his wife if she did not spend it at the place he had determined for this purpose?....................257
- Is it permissible for the husband to ask his wife to give him the cost of supporting her child who belongs to a former husband?.....................257

- Is a rich son entitled to support his old father,
his wife and brothers?...258
- Is it permissible to give one's relatives out of
one's Zakah and Kaffarah?......................................259
- What is the legal ruling on giving charity to
needy relatives?...259
- Nursing the baby...259
- Who is to nurse the baby? When is it permissible
for the nursing mother to demand for
financial support?...259
- When a mother takes her child and agrees with
her former husband that she will support their
child, but later she demanded for financial
support, is it permissible?..260
- Is it permissible for a father to oblige his son
to travel oversees without the son's
or mother's consent?..261
- Does the stepfather have the right to put the
daughter of his wife from another husband
under his custody?..262
- What about the son put under the custody
of his mother?...263
- Clarification and Comment......................................264
- Crimes and Penalties..265
- Unintentional and premeditated murder..................265
- When a group of people conspired to murder
a person but just one of them performed the
plot, will they be killed all or just the murderer?......267
- When a man beats another and later the beaten
person falls dead, what is the legal judgment

in this case?.............................268
- The penalty of adultery.........................268
- If the adulterer repented before due penalty
  is afflicted, is penalty canceled?...................268
- Do the viciousness of sins and the penalty
  of adultery increase in the blessed days?...............269
- The penalty of defaming people....................269
- When a man and his divorced wife defame
  his present wife and accuse her of adultery,
  is their claim accepted? Is the dowry
  of the present wife canceled?......................269
- Having hashish................................271
- Masturbation.................................271
- Is masturbation prohibited for men and
  women alike?...............................271

Translator's Note

Praise be to Allah, the Lord of the Worlds. Blessings and peace be upon our leader Muhammad, his family, his companions, and those who follow his guidance until the day of judgement.

Two major elements drove me to shoulder the responsibility of introducing a publication of such an imminent Imam Like Ibn Taymyah to those who learn Islam from English literature. The first is the author who, undoubtedly, needs no word that may attempt to crystallize his stance among other jurists, be they of his time or any other generation or place.

The second is the subject itself which grasps the interest of the people at any time. As man, woman enjoys an equal share as to rights, responsibilities and duties, all of which are best suiting her nature. Since science confirmed that woman is created with so many differences in her biological nature, physical capabilities and mental faculties, it would be unfair to assign her the same responsibilities, duties and rights as man.

In other words, there is a difference between sameness and equality. As man and woman are not the same in terms of biological nature, physical capabilities and mental faculties, so they are not the same and it would be injustice to deal with both the same. But to put into consideration this difference of nature is regarded as the core of justice and equality, the methodology adopted by Islam, the religion of the Creator of both man and woman.

As to Translation process, two things are considered. The first is the style which is free from literal translation which might lead to many misunderstandings on the part of reader especially when dealing with a classic style like that of Ibn Taymyah.

The second is the type of the fatwa. The source book comprises so many subjects that mostly concern man rather than woman. So the focus was centered on Fatwas which are confined to woman along with others that might appear to be interesting to woman.

We pray to Allah, the Exalted, to keep us on the right path to which He has guided us, and to bestow on us a blessing from Him, He is indeed the Most Merciful. Praise and gratitude be to Allah, the Lord of the worlds, and peace and blessings be upon prophet Muhammad, his family, his companions, and those who rightly follow them.

Purification

Altered water because of its being in a place for a long time

Q: What is the judgement of water if its color or taste is altered because of being in a place for a long period except its adore?

A: As to water being altered because of its being in a place for a long period, it is considered pure according to the majority view of scholars. As to the running Nile, if altered because of impurity mixed with it, it is impure. But if mixed with pure and impure elements and there is doubt as to whether it is pure or not, doubt is not sufficient basis to regard it as impure. In general seas don't change because of these elements, but if there is a certainty that it is changed by impure elements, it is impure. But if changed by pure elements, then the two traditional views are quoted here.

*   *   *

Men and women having Ghusl (purificatory bath) from the same container

Q: What about men and women having path from the same container?

A: There is no difference of opinion among jurists as to the permissibility of such action. Had it been the case, it is worthier to allow men and women to have path from one container respectively. And any one dislikes sharing Ghusl with another from the same container or to seek another bath to complete purification, is against the majority view.

*   *

Copper utensils inlayed with silver

Q: what about copper utensils inlayed with silver?

A: As to utensils inlayed with silver or its like, no harm if silver is little provided that needed and not of direct use. But if silver is too much, there are two views according to Alshafei and Ahmad. If silver is used for beautification and rings, it is permissible. As to utensils inlayed with gold, it is prohibited be it little or much.

There is a difference of opinion among the companions of Imam Ahmad as to the permissibility of performing ablution and purifacatory bath from gold and silver utensils. This difference is based on the rule of all things whose observance is obligatory while there are restrictions on seeking the permissibility like performing prayer in usurped land and prohibited clothes and performing pilgrimage with unlawful money. As to the matter in

24

question, there are two opinions according to the companions of Imam Ahmed. The first is tat it is permissible, which is the opinion of Alkharqi and others. The second is that it is not permissible, which the opinion of Abi Bakr.

The supporters of the first view drew two differences to support their view; the first is that prohibition here is separated from worship where the utensil is separated from the element of ablution which is different from the one who is wearing the prohibited or eating it or setting on it. In such case he is like one going to perform Friday prayer using usurped means.

Others deemed this difference weak saying that no difference could be claimed between putting the hand in the utensil or ladling with hands from it, and the prophet (may peace be upon him) said that the Billy of the drinker from gold and silver utensils is gargling with the hell fire. The second if prohibition touches the pillars and conditions of prayers, the prohibition is considered otherwise it will not affect its validity.

*   *

Circumcision of women

Q: What the rule of circumcision of women?

A: As man, circumcision should be observed to woman. Circumcision for woman consists of removing the prepuce from the clitoris (not the clitoris itself, as some mistakenly assert). In this regard the prophet (may peace be upon him) said: "Do it (circumcision) mildly without extreme, for it is healthy for both man and woman"

This hadith maintains that circumcision is meant only to make woman be able to control her lust, so it should be moderate without extreme. As to the circumcision of man, it consists of removing the prepuce from the penis to clean the filth that might gather in it.

*   *   *

Wiping over the head cover

Q: What about wiping the head cover?

A: Praise be to Allah, if there is any fear cold, she could wipe over the veil. It was reported that Um Salamah was used to wipe over her veil. She should wipe some of here hair along with the veil. But if there is no need to wipe over the veil, the scholars differ in such case.

*   *

Touching women

Q: Does touching women nullify ablution or not?

A: there are three views as to touching women.
The first which is the view of Imam Al-Shafie, which is regarded as the weakest, who maintains that ablution is

nullified by touching women even if they touch without sexual desire if the one of the opposite sex evokes sexual desire. This view is based on the Quranic verse that reads:
"or ye have been in contact with women"

The second view holds that touching doesn't nullify ablution even if sexual desire is evoked. This view is the view of Imam Ahmad.
The third, which is the view of Imam Malik, is that if touching is for the sake of sexual desire, ablution is nullified otherwise ablution still valid.
As to the view that holds ablution nullified by the act of touching a woman, it is against the consensus of companions and no text or Qias (analogical deduction) that may support this view. As to the verse that reads:
"or ye have been in contact with women",

Umar said that if touching means touching with the hand or kissing, it refers to touching for the sake of sexual desire like what is indicated in the following verse:
"but don't associate with your wives while ye are in retreate in the mosques."
Approaching women without sexual desire is not prohibited while approaching women in the mosque. The same also applied to the following verse:
"but if ye divorce them before consummation" and **"There is no blame on ye if divorce women before consummation"**.
According to the majority view of scholars if he divorces his wife before he approaches her with sexual desire, no waiting period, dower or the prohibition that based on

marriage relationship. But if he approaches her with sexual desire and practices marriage relationships, the matter is different and there is difference of opinion among jurists in the school of Imam Amad.

In light of the foregoing verses and the explanation regarding the word contacting, the view that claims touching in the verse **"or ye have been in contact with women"** refers to touching without sexual desire contradicts the references imbedded in the Quran and goes against its meaning in the general language of the people.

*　　*　　*

Touching the Holy Quran

The jurists are all agreed that it is forbidden to touch the Quran while one is in a state of impurity. He derives his support from a *hadith* in the two Sahihs in which it is stated that The Prophet (peace be upon him) sent a letter to Amr ibn Hazm in which he said: "The holy Quran is to be touched only by pure person". This is the view of Sulaiman Al-Faresey and Abd ullah bin Umar and all companions.

*　　*　　*

Carrying the Holy Quran

Q: What about carrying the holy Quran in the state of impurity?

A: It should be carried shrouded with any thing like

clothes or the like, be it confined to man or not.

*   *   *

Reading the Qur'an during puerperium (Nifas)

Q: What about a woman in puerperium: is she allowed to read the Qur'an while in confinement? Is she allowed to engage in sexual intercourse before the forty days are over? If the forty days are over but the woman has not performed the purificatory bath, is she allowed to engage in sexual intercourse?

A: The four scholars unanimously agreed that it is unlawful for a woman to engage in sexual intercourse before the bleeding stops. If the bleeding stops before the forty days are over, she is to perform the purificatory bath and pray. However, her husband is not allowed to copulate with her before the forty days are over. As for reading the Qur'an, if she does not fear forgetting the verses she memorized, she is not to read the Qur'an.

However, if she does fear forgetting them, she is allowed to read the Qur'an, according to some of the scholars. It is unanimously agreed that when the bleeding stops and the woman performs the purificatory bath, she can read the Qur'an and pray. If she cannot perform the purificatory bath due to the absence of water or on account of some disease, she is to perform the dry ablution instead which is equivalent to the purificatory bath.

Prayer

Making up missed prayers

Q: Should a man who missed many prayers make them up along with their optional (*Sunnah*) prayers, or is he to make up the obligatory prayers only ? And are they to be made up any time of the day?

A: Immediacy in making up missed prayers is more important than occupying oneself with making up optional prayers. Yet, if the prayers missed are few in number, making up optional prayers is recommended.

When the Prophet, peace and blessings be upon him, and his companions overslept and missed the dawn(*Fajr*) prayer, during *Hunain* battle, they made up the obligatory and optional prayer, and when he missed the prayer during the trench battle, he made up only the obligatory prayers and not the optional ones. Missed prayers can be made up any time of day. The Prophet, peace and blessings be upon him, says: **"Whoever finds one *rak'ah* (unit) at dawn before the rising of the sun, he in fact finds the dawn prayer."**

Is making up missed prayer better

Than performing optional prayer ?

Q: which is better, making up missed prayers or performing optional prayers ?

A: If a man has missed an obligatory prayer, making it up is more important than occupying oneself with performing optional prayers.

*   *   *

Woman's ornament

Q: What about a woman's outfit and whether she is allowed to display it?

A: In prayer, a woman is allowed to display outward, but not inward, ornaments. The predecessors had disagreed as to what outward ornament is. Ibn Masoud and his supporters stated it was clothes, whereas Ibn Abass and his supporters mentioned it was the face and the hands, such as the kohl (eye liner) and rings.

Based on these two views, scholars disagreed whether it is allowed to look at a strange woman. According to Abu Haneifa and Ashafe'ei, driven by no sexual appetite, a man is allowed to look at a woman's hands and face.

According to Ahmad's view, a man is not allowed to. According to Malek, the whole body of a woman is considered private parts, right down to her nails.

The conclusion

Ornaments are of two types; outward and inward. Allah has allowed a woman to display her ornaments to people other than her husband and her prohibited affinities.

Before the verse obligating a woman to take the veil was revealed, women used to go out wearing no outer garments (*jilbab*) and men were able to see their hands and faces, since a woman was allowed to show both her hands and face then. Consequently, it was not unlawful for a man to look at them as she was allowed to display them.

When Allah, exalted be He, revealed the verse obligating a woman to take the veil, **"O Prophet ! Tell thy wives and daughters, and the believing women, that they should cast their outer garments over their persons (when abroad)"** (Al Ahzab: 59), women became forbidden to look at.   That was when the Prophet married Zaynab bent Gahsh, he drew curtains and forbade women to be looked at.   When he married Safeya bent Hoiay, a year later, i.e. in the year when the battle of Khaibar took place, people said: If he forbade that she be looked at, she would be one of the mothers of the believers, otherwise she would be one of those whom his right hand possesses. So he ordered that she be veiled.

Allah ordered that women be not asked questions except from behind a veil, and ordered that the Prophet's wives and daughters as well as the believing women should cast their outer garments over their persons. This outer garment or *jilbab* is a sheet of cloth or what Ibn Masoud and others refer to as raiment, and which is generally referred to by people as loincloth, that is the large loincloth covering her head and her whole body.

Abu Obayda and others narrated that women used to hang it down on their heads so that only their eyes could be seen. Similarly, women who used to cover their faces.

According to the authentic book, **"And the *Muhrima* (a woman in the state of *Ihram* [sanctity]) should not cover her face, and should not wear gloves."** So, if women are ordered to wear the outer garment (*jilbab*), which entails covering the face, the face and the hands are therefore understood to be among the ornaments that she is ordered not to display before strangers. In addition to that, strangers are allowed to look at all else with the exception of outside clothes.

Ibn Masoud mentioned the latter, whereas Ibn Abass mentioned the former. The verse allows a woman to display ornaments to her prohibited affinities and others, while the Prophet's saying only permits it to the prohibited affinities. The verse mentions **"their women, their slaves whom their right hands possess, or male servants free**

of physical need", though a woman is not allowed to travel with any of them.

Allah says, **"their women"** so as to exclude the disbelieving women, for a disbelieving woman is not to deliver a Muslim woman, nor to enter a bathroom with her. However, Jewish women used to walk in on A'isha and others and they saw her face and hands, which men were not allowed to see.

Thus, the face and hands are understood to be among the inward ornaments and displaying them would depend on who is to see them. Allah says, **"they should cast their outer garments over their persons (when abroad)"**, meaning a woman is to cover her neck, and so necklaces and the like are considered to be among the inward and not the outward ornaments.

*   *   *

Concealing women's private parts from men and women

Q: What about concealing women's private parts from men and women.?

A: Allah's Prophet, peace and blessings be upon him, said, **"A man should not see the private parts of another man, and a woman should not see the private parts of another woman."** He also said, **"Conceal your private parts except from your wife and from whom your right hand possesses (slave-girl). I then asked: (what should we do), if the people are assembled together? He**

replied, If it is within your power that no one looks at it, then no one should look at it. I then asked: If one of us is alone (what should he do)? He replied, Allah is more entitled than people that bashfulness should be seen to Him."

Concerning children, the Prophet said, **"Command your children to pray when they become seven years old and beat them for it (prayer) when they become ten years old; and arrange their beds (to sleep) separately."** Thus, looking at as well as touching the private parts of others is forbidden on account of the obscenity and indecency of that.

As for concealing women from men, this is on account of the libido involved and this falls into two categories. There is yet a third category to be observed in prayer; if a woman prays alone, she must wear a veil, whereas she is allowed to walk bare-headed at home. Thus, taking the veil during prayer is out of reverence to Allah.

Likewise, man is not allowed to walk around his house naked, even if he is alone and at night, nor to pray naked. even if he is alone. Therefore, wearing clothes during prayer is not to conceal oneself from people, as this is an entirely different matter. Hence, a man can cover certain parts of his body while praying which he is allowed to leave uncovered when not praying.

Conversely, he is allowed to leave uncovered in prayer what he must conceal from men. The former refers to the shoulders, for instance, as the Prophet, peace and blessings be upon him, forbade a man to pray in a single garment that does not cover his shoulders. This is a must out of reverence to prayer, whereas man is allowed to uncover his shoulders before other men when not praying.

Similarly, a woman must wear a veil while praying, as the Prophet, peace and blessings be upon him, said, "Allah does not accept the prayer of a woman who has reached puberty unless she wears a veil." However, a woman does not have to wear a veil before her husband or her prohibited affinities. A woman is allowed to display her inward ornaments before them, but is not allowed to uncover her head before them or any others while praying.

*   *   *

Showing the face, the hands, and the feet before strangers

On the other hand, a woman is not allowed to display her face, hands and feet before strangers, according to the most valid of the two opinions, unlike what was followed before the verse was nullified by Allah. She is only to display her clothes. However, she is not to cover them during prayer, as all Muslims unanimously agree. They can be displayed in prayer according to the majority of scholars, such as Abu Haneifa, Ashafei and others.

Likewise, according to Abu Haneifa, the feet can be displayed, which is the opinion most likely to be correct. According to A'isha, the feet are among the outward ornaments, she said, **" that they should not display their beauty and ornaments except what (must ordinarily) appear thereof ."** (Al Nur: 31) She also said, **"The toe ring is a ring made of silver for the toes."** Narrated by Abu Hatem, which proves that women used to show their feet, their hands and faces and they also used to hang down their garments so that if a woman walks her feet could be seen. Women did not use to wear shoes and so covering their feet in prayer would be an enormous inconvenience.

Om Salamah said, "A woman can pray in a shift that reaches down and covers the top of her feet" so that if she kneels down in prostration, the sole of her feet could be seen.

In conclusion:

It was proved both by the Qur'an and by the unanimity of scholars that a woman does not have to wear a loose garment that covers her body even if she prays at home. However, she must wear it when she goes out. When she prays at home, her hands and face can be seen, as the private parts in prayer are not related to that private parts prohibited to be looked at.

Ibn Masoud, may Allah be pleased with him, said that outward ornaments are clothes. However, he did not say that the entire body of the woman is considered private parts, right down to her nails. This is rather the opinion of Ahmad. So, this is a must for the validity of prayer. Scholars call this (The chapter on covering the private parts). This is not to quote the Prophet. Likewise, neither the Qur'an nor the tradition of the Prophet refer to the fact that what we cover in prayer is considered private parts. Allah, the Almighty, says, " **O the children of Adam! Wear your beautiful apparel at every time and place of prayer".** (Al A'raf: 31) The Prophet forbade man to walk around his house naked, which, of necessity, applies to prayer.

*　　*　　*

Does a woman have to cover her hands in prayer?

Ordering women to cover their hands in prayer is far-fetched. When a woman kneels down in prostration, she kneels down with her face and her hands as well. In the days when the Prophet, peace and blessings be upon him, lived, women used to wear garments. They used to work in their garments. Thus, a women would show her hands when grinding seeds, kneading bread and baking it. Had covering the hands been a must in prayer, the Prophet would have stated so. The same thing applies to the feet.

However, a woman is only ordered to wear a veil together with the garment. Hence, women used to pray in their garments and veils. As for the garment that the woman used to let down, she asked the Prophet, peace and blessings be upon him, about it and he said, **"A hand span."** They asked, **"What if it leaves their legs uncovered?"** He said, **"Then the length of a forearm and let them not increase it."**

The Prophet was also asked about the woman who drags her garment behind her over dirty places, he said, **"What follows purifies it."** Yet, a woman does not wear such dragging shifts at home. Likewise, women later began to wear slippers to cover their legs when they went out, yet they never wore them at home. That's why they asked, **"What if it leaves their legs uncovered?"** Hence, the purpose was to cover the leg, because if the garments were ankle-high, the leg could be seen while walking.

It has also been narrated that the Prophet said that if the woman had no appropriate garment to wear, she is to stay home. Muslim women used to pray at home, yet the Prophet, peace be upon him, said, **"Do not stop Allah's women slaves from going to Allah's mosques yet it is better for them to pray at home."** However, the woman was not ordered to cover her feet with slippers or with socks. Nor was she ordered to cover her hands with gloves or anything of the sort. This, in turn, proves that neither her feet nor her hands are to be covered in prayer unless there are strange men around.

It was also narrated, **"The angels do not look at inward ornaments.   So if a woman takes off her veil and her garment, they do not look at her."** Khadija once narrated one of the Prophet's sayings on this issue.

Therefore, a woman is only ordered to wear a veil when praying. Similarly, when a man prays in a loose shift, he is ordered to cover his private parts and shoulders. A man's shoulders are considered equivalent to woman's head, as a man prays in a shift or the like. When in a state of sanctity (*Ihram*), a man is not to wear a shift, and a woman is not to cover her face or wear gloves either. Similarly, a man is not to cover his head.

Scholars belonging   to Imam Ahmad's school differed concerning a   woman's face. Some said, it is to be treated like a man's head and so is not to be covered. Others maintained, a woman's face is equivalent to a man's hands and so must not be covered with special face veils that were tailored to   its size, which is the opinion believed to be most valid, as the Prophet, peace and blessings be upon him, only forbade women to wear gloves and face veils.

Women used to hang down on their faces pieces of cloth to cover them from men, without actually clothing the face since her face is equivalent to her hands and to a man's hands. As previously mentioned, the entire body of a woman is considered private parts. Thus, she is allowed to cover her hands and face, but not using especially tailored close-fitting clothes. Likewise, a man is not to wear trousers but is to wear a loincloth.

*   *   *

The uncovering of a woman's hair during prayer

Q: Would woman's prayer be invalidated if some of her hair was uncovered during prayer?

A: If only a small portion of her hair or her body was uncovered, she does not have to repeat the prayer, according to the majority of scholars, namely Abu Haneifa and Ahmad. Yet, if much of her body or her hair was uncovered, she is to repeat the prayer, according to all scholars, the four Imams and others.

*   *   *

A woman praying with the surface of her foot uncovered

Q: Is a woman allowed to perform prayer with the surface of her foot uncovered?

41

A: This issue is debatable among scholars. Abu Haneifa maintains that she can, though others believe otherwise.

*   *   *

Sewing silk for men and women and getting paid for it.

Q: What about pure silk: Is a tailor allowed to sew it for men? Will the money he will be paid for the job be unlawful? Will he be condemned for it? Are clothes not made of silk but decorated with it allowed to be sold? Is silk allowed to be sewn for women?

A: It is unlawful to sew silk into unlawful outfits such as pure silk outfits for men when it is not war time, and not for purposes of remedy. This would be regarded as taking part in sinning, which is similar to manufacturing gold and silver utensils, according to the most valid opinion among the majority of scholars.

This also applies to whatever involves photography, resulting in its being unlawful to use. Again this applies to the making of wine. Money paid in return for unlawful doings are equally unlawful. However, sewing silk for whomever are allowed to wear silk, such as women, is lawful, even if a tailor touches it during sewing. Similarly, this applies to molding gold and silver into whatever is lawful to use.

Silk may be used in decorating men's clothes. Likewise.

according to the Prophetic tradition, it is allowed to edge outfits with silk stripes that are only five or six centimeters in width at most and the Prophet, peace be upon him, had a jubbah edged with silk.

*   *   *

Women's wearing kaffiehs

Q: Are women allowed to wear kaffiehs? What are the criteria relied on in judging women's imitating men's wear? Should the criteria be based on the norms of the Prophet's days or are they to vary according to varying ages?

A: Kaffiehs which do not cover the hair that is hanging down loose are among men's wear. So for women to wear them is to imitate men. Dressing this way may have been pioneered by women who meant to imitate men. A slave women may wear her hair in a single braid that hangs down between her shoulders, letting down locks of hair on both sides of her head, then wears a head turban in order to look like men. Though some free women may follow suit, they, in doing so, wrongfully imitate men.

Authentic books tell in detail how the Prophet has cursed women who imitate men and men who imitate women. He was also narrated to have said, **"Effeminate men are cursed, and so are women who imitate men."** The Prophet also ordered effeminate men to be banished. Ashafei', Ahmad and others asserted that they are to banished, maintaining that according to the Prophetic tradition, banishment is the punishment for adultery and effeminacy.

According to Sahih Muslim, he said, **"I have not yet come across two categories of Muslims who will be tortured in Hellfire: women who are dressed yet naked, and who walk and strut with a swinging gait, they shall not be admitted into heaven, nor will they ever come close to it, and men who walk around with whips that look like tails of cows wherewith they lash Allah's servants.**

He (may peace be upon hime) was narrated to have passed by Om Salamah's and saw her tying a band around her head, so he said, **"O Om Salamah, tie it only once not twice"**. He explained **"women who are dressed yet naked"** as women who wear garments that do not cover their bodies. They are hence dressed, yet still naked. Or women who wear transparent clothes that show their bodies or tight outfits that display the curves of their bodies like their bottoms, their arms and the sort. Women are supposed to wear loose gowns that cover their bodies and do not display the size of their organs.

*   *   *

The criteria of imitating the other sex

Hence appears the criteria based on which the Prophet, peace be upon him, forbade men to imitate women and women to imitate men. This has nothing to do with what men or women choose to wear or their habits of dressing, because had this been the case, it would have been acceptable to have a nation where men were accustomed to wearing veils that cover their heads, faces and necks and gowns that would hang down loosely from their heads downwards displaying only the eyes and where women were in the habit of wearing turbans and tight manly coats and the like. However, this runs contrary to the Qur'an, the Prophet's sayings and the unanimously agreed upon opinion.

Allah, exalted be He, says, addressing women, **"that they should draw their veils over their bosoms and not display their beauty except to their husbands"**
He also says, **"Tell thy wives and daughters, and the believing women, that they should cast their outer garments over their persons (when abroad): that is most convenient, that they should be known (and such) and not molested."** Also **"and make not a dazzling display, like that of the former times of Ignorance:"**

Had the difference between men and women's wear been based on their habits and tastes, it would not have been a must for them to cast their outer garments over their persons, nor to draw their veils over their bosoms, nor would it have been forbidden to "make a dazzling display, like that of the former times of Ignorance" since those were the habits of people then.

However, no particular outfit is made obligatory based on the usual costume of the Prophet's days or the habits of men and women's wear then, so that none but this particular outfit would be permissible. Women in those days used to wear gowns with trains that would trail behind them whereas men were ordered to wear only ankle-length outfits.

Thus, when the Prophet forbade men to wear long outfits that would hang down, he was asked, **"What about women?"** He said, **"They are to wear garments that would hang down only a few inches, i.e. equal to the span of the hand."** They said, **"Their legs would hence be shown."** He said, **"Then it should be an ell and no more."**

That is why when a women has her gown trailing behind her over filthy places then over clean places, her gown is immediately made clean, according to a host of scholars belonging to Ahmad's school. This trailing gown is thus regarded as similar to the shoes that are in constant contact with filth and is thus made clean by rubbing it against hard surfaces, just the same way that liquids are made clean since they both come in contact with filth.

Apart from that, if a woman wears trousers or huge hard

shoes over which a long loose garment hangs down in such a way that does not display the size of her feet, this will have achieved the intended purpose. Conversely, soft close-fitting shoes that display the size of the feet are among men's wear.

Similarly, a women is allowed to wear manly coats and furs if she needs to in order to warm up in cold weather. So if it is claimed that women then did not use to wear furs, the answer will be that this depends on whether there is a need to. Cold countries call for thick clothing for warmth, which are not required in hot countries.

Thus, the difference between men and women's wear is based on what is fit for each of them and what will enable each of them to fulfill what they are commanded to do. Women are commanded to take the veil and not to show their beauty publicly.

They are thus not allowed to call for prayer, to make devotional calls (*talbiya*), to go up the Safa and Marwa Mounts nor to undress in *Ihram* (the state of sanctity) the way men are commanded to.

Man, on the other hand, is commanded to uncover his head and not to wear conventional tight-fitting clothes, such as shirts, trousers, shower robes, nor shoes. However, since he needs to cover his private parts and wear some clothes to walk around in, he is permitted to wear trousers if he cannot find shifts and to wear shoes if he cannot find slippers.

These are therefore alternatives to meet the general need in contrast to what man needs to meet some private needs such as cold weather or illness, cases that call for paying a ransom. That is why Abu Haneifa ruled out this deduction and many disagreed with it depending on the authentic Prophetic sayings and because of the difference between both cases.

*   *   *

Women's wearing turbans

Q: Is it unlawful for women to wear turbans? What kind of turbans are women recommended to wear? Are they allowed to wear close-fitting shoes?

A: These turbans that women wear are unlawful. The prophet, peace
be upon him, is narrated to have said, **"I have not yet come across two categories of Muslims who will be tortured in Hellfire: women who are dressed yet naked, and who walk and strut with a swinging gait, they shall not be admitted into heaven, nor will they ever come close to it, and men who walk around with whips that look like tails of cows wherewith they lash Allah's servants."**

*   *   *

Is a Christian woman to be buried among Muslims?

Q: A Christian woman was married to a Muslim, and was seven months pregnant when she died. Is she to be buried in Muslim's or Christians' cemetery?

A: She is not to be buried either in Muslims' or in Christians' cemetery since both a Muslim and a Christian are involved and a Muslim is not to buried among the disbelievers, nor is a disbeliever to be buried among Muslims.

The Christian woman is to be buried alone with her back facing the Qibla, since the baby's face is towards his mother's back. Burying the woman this way, the Muslim baby will be facing the Qibla. A baby is born Muslim if his father is Muslim, even if his mother is not, as unanimously agreed on by all scholars.

*   *

Zakah
Zakah of Jewelry

Q: Is jewelry subject to Zakah?

A: According to Malek, Allayeth, Ashafei', Ahmad and Abu Obayd, no Zakah is due on women's jewelry. On the other hand, Marwei Ibn Omar, Ibn Masoud, Ibn Abbas, Ibn Omar and others maintain that Zakah I due on women's jewelry.

49

Regarding men's adornments, no Zakah is due on lawful adornments such as swords adornments and silver rings. As for unlawful adornments, such as gold and silver utensils, no Zakah is due. Concerning adornments that were a point of controversy such as helmets and shields adornments, obligating Zakah was again a bone of contention. According to Malek and Ashafei' , Zakah is due on them and they are declared unlawful to keep.

Abu Haneifa and Ahmad declared them lawful adornments provided they are made of silver. As for horses adornments, such as saddles and bridles, the majority of scholars maintain that Zakah is ordained on them.

Malek, Ashafei' and Ahmad proclaimed them unlawful to keep. Likewise, Zakah is due on inkwells, kohl containers and things of the sort, be they made of silver or gold.

*　　*　　*

Zakah on a woman's dowry

Q: If a woman is unable to demand her dowry of her husband for years lest this should cause a falling-out, then she is compensated for it by an estate or she is paid the full dowry years later. Is she to pay due Zakah for the previous years or is she only to pay a year's Zakah 12 months after she was paid her dowry?

A: Scholars differed on this issue.

Some maintained: Zakah of the previous years is to be paid, be the husband rich or poor, according to one of the two opinions in Ashafei and Ahamd's schools.

Others believed: Zakah of the previous years is due only if the husband is rich and if she has actually been paid the dowry.   Yet, if this is not the case, no Zakah is due, according to the second opinion in their school.

Others claimed: Zakah is due for only one year, according to Malek and one of the opinions in Ahmad's school.

Others thought: No Zakah is due at all, according to Abu Haneifa and one of the opinions in Ahamd's school.

The most far-fetched opinion is the one obligating paying Zakah for the previous years, even when a woman has not been paid her dowry. This opinion is invalid. Ordaining Zakah on what one has not paid is against the Sharia. Besides, with the years, Zakah can exceed the original sum of   money. Moreover, if the appointed sum on which Zakah is due (*Nisab*) became less and Zakah is due only on this appointed sum, it would be difficult to figure out the Zakah to be paid.

The opinion believed to be most valid is the one that deem Zakah not due except after a whole year as of the date of payment or the one obligating one year's Zakah to be paid upon getting the dowry. This opinion obviously rests on solid grounds, and is adopted by Abu Haneifa, Malek and a group of scholars belonging to Ahmad's school.

*   *

Can the grandmother be a legitimate recipient of Zakah if in debt?

Q: What about a poor woman who was in debt and had in her custody young grandchildren (her daughter's children) who had money. Are they allowed to pay Zakah to their grandmother? Does she come first on the list of worthy recipients?

A: According to the most valid of scholars' opinions, they are allowed to pay their Zakah to her or to any of their relatives so they could pay back their debt.

As for paying her the Zakah to help her afford their daily bread, if she can afford the expenses of raising them or others, she is not to be paid the Zakah. However, if she needs Zakah, she is thus a legitimate recipient and is morality can others.

Fasting

Is a pregnant woman, who is in no pain, allowed not to fast for the safety of her baby?

Q: If a pregnant woman was spotting on regular basis and midwives advised her not to fast for the safety of the baby, yet she was in no pain, would she be allowed not to fast?

A: If a pregnant woman fears for her baby, she is allowed not to fast provided that she fast an equal number of days later and to distribute a rotl of bread and accompanying food among poor people equal in number to the days she did not fast in Ramadan.

What is a fasting Muslim allowed to do? What would break his fasting and what would not?

Q: What about rinsing the mouth, sniffing water, tooth cleansers, tasting food, vomiting, bleeding, wearing perfume and kohl?

A: Scholars unanimously agree that a fasting Muslim can rinse his mouth and sniff water. The Prophet, peace be upon him, and his companions used to rinse their mouths and sniff water while fasting. Yet, he said to Loqayt Ibn Sabrh, **"Thoroughly sniff water unless you are fasting."** He did not forbid him to sniff water but forbade him to overdo it.   Likewise, it is unanimously agreed that it is permissible to use the tooth cleanser.   However, they differed as to whether it is not commendable to use it after noon.   Yet, no evidence based on the Qur'an or the Prophetic tradition was found sufficient to pose restraints on the general applicability of verses or the Prophet's sayings dealing with the tooth cleanser.

Tasting food: is not recommendable if uncalled for but does not break one's fasting, unlike rinsing one's mouth which is called for.
Vomiting: if one deliberately causes himself to vomit, it breaks one's fasting.   However, if one vomits against one's will, it does not.

Wearing perfume: does not break one's fasting as unanimously agreed on.

Bleeding: bleeding that cannot be helped such as bleeding induced by injuries, or cases of brandymenorrhoea or nose bleeding does not break one's fasting.   Yet, it is unanimously agreed that menstruation and postnatal bleeding breaks a woman's fasting.

As for having one's blood drawn, it has been debatable among scholars whether this breaks one's fasting, yet it is generally believed to do.   Similarly, bloodletting or phlebotomy has equally been debatable. According to one opinion, it is regarded as equivalent to having one's blood drawn and so does break one's fasting.

Concerning kohl, Ahmad and Malek believe that like perfume, it breaks one's fasting only if it reaches inside one's head, whereas Abu Haneifa and Ashafei' believe it does not.

*   *   *

A man who could not fast or pray right before his death.

Q: A man was incapacitated by illness during Ramadan and could not fast or pray, then died. His parents are still alive though. If they fast and pray for him, will they have performed the obligation for him? Does he have to explicitly request this in his will?

A: If the man took ill and could not perform the obligations, his parents only have to feed poor people in compensation. As for prayer, no one has to pray on behalf of another. However, if one of his parents voluntarily prays or fasts on behalf of their dead son, he is rewarded for it.

*

Refraining from going to extremes in worshipping Allah

Q: What about going to extremes in worshipping Allah?

A: A man heard the Prophet, peace be upon in, as saying, **"David's prayer was the most pleasing to Allah, and David's fasting was the most pleasing to Allah; he used to sleep half of the night, pray its third and sleep its sixth and he used to fast every other day."**

So he pledged to fast every other day and continued to do so for over a year. The man was married and had children, which required him to preserve his health and vitality. The man next grew keener on memorizing verses of the Qur'an, so he kept learning verses and repeating them every day.

He also got in the habit of praying a large portion of the night and grew more enthusiastic on worshipping Allah. As a result, the difficulty of fasting together with the difficulty of repeating and memorizing verses of the Qur'an coupled with the exhaustion entailed by devoted worshipping of Allah, though he was a young man with zest and vitality, all resulted in a state of distraction. severe headache and slow comprehension in the sense that he became unable to grasp the meaning of whatever he hears. This exhaustion could be seen in his sunken eyes.

Yet, his devotion in worshipping Allah brought some light into his life. The man refused to quit fasting in order to honor the pledge he made to Allah and for fear that this light in his life should fade away.

Whenever any of the well-versed men of religion tried to dissuade him from persisting in it, he would say, I want to kill myself for the sake of Allah. So does this fasting, given the state he is in, please Allah, exalted be He? Or is it not recommendable? Is the man entitled to make such a pledge and can he pay money in expiation for violating it? Should he not preserve his physical and mental health in order to be able to perform the obligations and support his children so as to please Allah? Would not his persistence in doing so incur Allah's wrath on the grounds that the man is wearing himself out by forcing himself to do what he does not have to do?

* * *

A woman going on a pilgrimage without an unmarriageable kin.

Q: Can a woman go on a pilgrimage unaccompanied by an **unmarriageable kin**?

A: If the woman is elderly, no longer menstruates, has given up all hope of getting married and has no unmarriageable kin, she can go on a pilgrimage in the company of someone she trusts, according to Malek, Ashafei' and one of the two opinions in Ahmad's school.

Can a woman go on a pilgrimage on behalf of another?

Q: Can a woman go on a pilgrimage on behalf of another?

A: Scholars unanimously agreed that a woman can perform a pilgrimage on behalf of another woman, be she her daughter or any other woman. Similarly, according to the four Imams and the majority of scholars, a woman can perform the pilgrimage on behalf of a man. The Prophet, peace be upon him, ordered a woman from Kath'am to perform the pilgrimage on behalf of her father, when she said, **"O Allah's Prophet, Allah has obligated pilgrimage on His servants when my father was an elderly man. So the Prophet, peace be upon him, ordered her to perform the pilgrimage on her father's behalf."** However, it would be more whole for a man to do it.

*　　*　　*

Can a woman who has already performed the pilgrimage go on a pilgrimage on behalf of a dead person and be paid for it?

Q: what about a woman who has already been on a pilgrimage and was asked to perform the pilgrimage on behalf of a dead person in return for money. Would she be allowed to do so?

A: She is allowed to perform the pilgrimage for a dead person in return for money to be accepted with the intention of performing the obligation on his behalf, as unanimously agreed on. However, if the money is paid for hiring the woman, scholars were of two opinions:

The first: Ashafei' maintained that she can take the money. That second: Abu Haneifa maintained that she cannot. If this woman who has already been on a pilgrimage intends to perform the obligation on behalf of the dead person, she would be rewarded for it. However, if she was solely after the money, she would be deprived of any reward.

* * *

Circumambulation of the Sacred House made by a menstruating woman

Q: What is the judgment of a woman who circumambulates the Sacred House in her menses?

A: According to one of the two opinions of the scholars who claim that purification is obligatory for circumambulation, if a menstruating woman, or any one who is ritually impure due to seminal discharge, minor impurity i.e. not taking ablution, or because of carrying impurity in general, circumambulates the Sacred House, it will be sufficient for him/her and will be required to sacrifice either a sheep in the case of minor impurity or a she-camel in the case of menstruation or impurity due to seminal discharge.

Forbidding a menstruating woman to circumambulation may be accounted for the fact that circumambulation resembles Prayer, or because she is forbidden to enter the mosque in the case of circumambulation, exactly as in the case of observing I'tikaf [seclusion for a certain time in the mosque for devotion]. Allah the Almighty said to Prophet Abraham [Ibrahim] what means: "...**and sanctify My House for those who compass it round, or stand up, or bow, or prostrate themselves (therein in prayer)."** (22:26)

As Allah ordered Prophet Abraham to purify the sanctify i.e. purify the Sacred House to accommodate the doers of the above-mentioned kinds of devotion, a menstruating woman is forbidden to enter it.

The scholars, however, agreed on the opinion that circumambulation cannot be treated like Prayer in terms of what is lawful and what is prohibited, and that circumambulation cannot be annulled by the same acts that nullify Prayer, such as eating, drinking, speaking what is alien to the words of Prayer, etc.

For those who hold that a menstruating woman is forbidden to circumambulate the Sacred House because she

is not permitted to enter it at the first place, not because
that she is not permitted to make circumambulation itself,
they   claim   that   purity   is   not   a   condition   for
circumambulation,   rather   a   menstruating   woman can
circumambulate the Sacred House in case of necessity, as
she is permitted to enter the mosque in case of necessity.

Allah   ordered   Prophet   Abraham   to   purify   the Sacred
House to accommodate those who circumambulate it, those
who observe I'tikaf in it, and those who perform Prayer in
it.   According to the agreement of Muslim scholars, purity
from   minor   impurity   i.e.   making   ablution,   is   not a
prerequisite for observing I'tikaf.

A woman who observes I'tikaf then has her menses during
her stay in the mosque may continue her stay if she is
driven by necessity. As for the phrase **"...or bow, or
prostrate themselves (therein in prayer),"** it indicates
that   the   observers   of   Prayer,   for   which   purity   is a
prerequisite,   according   to   the   unanimous   agreement of
Muslim scholars.   However, a menstruating woman is not
required to perform Prayer, neither the Prayers in the time
of her menstruation, nor the Prayers she had missed before
she becomes menstruating.

Another question is raised with regard to one who
circumambulates the Sacred Hose, shall he be treated like
one who observes I'tikaf or like one who performs Prayer
in terms of the requirement of purity? This question

opened a large scale exercise of *Ijtihad* [exercise of discretionary opinion based on Qur'an and Sunnah]. As for the saying that "circumambulation of the Sacred House is like Prayer," it is ascribed to Ibn 'Abbas, not to the Prophet (peace be upon him). Some jurists reported Ibn 'Abbas as saying: If one circumambulates the Sacred House while being ritually impure due to seminal discharge, he will be required to offer a sacrifice.

No doubt what is meant here is that circumambulation resembles Prayer in some aspects, but not that it is a kind of Prayer, for which purity is a must. The same applies to the report: "If any of you attends the mosque, he should not interlock his hands, as he will be regarded in Prayer," and the report: "A servant will be considered in a continuous Prayer, so long as he is bound by the manners of Prayer, waiting for the next Prayer, or heading for Prayer."

Briefly put, according to the agreement of Muslim scholars, a woman should not circumambulate the Sacred House, unless she is ritually pure, as much as she can. If she reaches the Sacred House while being menstruating, she should not circumambulate it. But she can attend 'Arafah and perform all rituals other than circumambulation. She should wait until she becomes ritually pure, then make circumambulation, if she can stay. If she is obliged to circumambulate the Sacred House in her menses, it will sufficient for her. This is the soundest of the two opinions ascribed to Muslim scholars.

Attending 'Arafah by a menstruating woman

Q: What is the judgment of a menstruating woman who attends 'Arafah?

A: A menstruating woman can attend 'Arafah. One can attend 'Arafah walking or riding. The best of these is determined according to the conditions of people. If riding is preferable to a man, so that the people, who are in need of him, may see him, or because walking is difficult for him, he may attend 'Arafah while riding, as the Prophet (peace be upon him) once attended 'Arafah while riding.

*   *   *

A weak woman who spends the night in Muzdalifah

Q: What is the judgment of a weak woman who spends the night in Muzdalifah?

A: According to the Prophetic Sunnah, a male pilgrim should spend the night in Muzdalifah and wait until it is dawn, then perform the Morning Prayer and attend the *Mash'ar Al-Haram*, in which he should stay until he leaves before sunset. If the pilgrim is of the weak, such as women and children, he/she should hasten to Mina after the set of the moon. Strong pilgrims should not leave Muzdalifah unless after the break of the dawn, performing the Morning Prayer, standing by Muzdalifah, since all the area of Muzdalifah is a station, however, standing by Mount Qazah is more preferable. There lies the place that most jurists call *Al-Mash'ar Al-Haram*.

*   *   *

Circumambulation made by one who is ritually impure due to menstruation, seminal discharge or due to minor impurity i.e. not making ablution

Q: What is the judgment of one who circumambulates the Sacred House while being ritually impure due to menstruation, seminal discharge or due to minor impurity i.e. not making ablution?

A: It was reported after the Prophet (peace be upon him) that he said: "A menstruating woman performs all rituals except circumambulation of the Sacred House." He (peace be upon him) said to 'A'ishah, who was in her menses: "Do what a pilgrim does, except for circumambulation of the Sacred House." When the Prophet was told that his wife Safiyah menstruated, he exclaimed: "Shall she hinder us (from performing our rituals)? When he was told that she made the Ifadah circumambulation, he said: "This should not have been done." It was reported that the Prophet (peace be upon him) appointed Abu Bakr on the occasion of pilgrimage in the year 9 A.H. to announce people that it is not permissible for a pilgrim to circumambulate the Sacred House while being nude.

It was not reported that he (peace be upon him) ordered those who circumambulate the Sacred House to make ablution or avoid impurities, while he ordered those who were going to Prayer to make ablution. The forbiddance of circumambulation by a menstruating woman was thus because of maintaining the sanctity of the mosque, as a menstruating woman is not permitted to stay in it, while circumambulation requires a stay in the mosque, or because it is totally forbidden to enter the mosque, either as passing by it or staying in it.

The forbiddance of a menstruating woman to circumambulate the Sacred House might also because of the prohibition of circumambulation on the part of a menstruating woman, just as she is prohibited to perform Prayer or observe Fasting, which is proved by Qur'an, Sunnah and the consensus of opinion, to touch the Holy Qur'an, according to most scholars, or to recite the Holy Qur'an, according to one of the two variant opinions of scholars.

Those who prohibited the recitation of the Holy Qur'an by a menstruating woman, such as the famous opinion of Imam Ahmad and the opinions of Imam Al-Shafi'i and Imam Abu Hanifah, disputed over the permissibility of recitation of the Holy Qur'an by a menstruating woman and one who suffers from puerperal bleeding before washing but after the cessation of bleeding into three opinions:

1. It is permissible for a woman to recite the Holy Qur'an after the cessation of menstrual or puerperal blood, and before the ritual bathing. This is the chosen opinion of the judge Abu Ya'la and the surface meaning of the opinion of Imam Ahmad.

2. Recitation of the Holy Qur'an by a woman after the cessation of menstrual or puerperal blood, and before performing a ritual bathing is totally forbidden.

3. It is permissible for a woman to recite the Holy Qur'an following childbirth, while a menstruating woman is prohibited.

As for the prohibition of a menstruating woman to enter the mosque or pass by it, it may be a prohibition of each act respectively, i.e. staying or passing by the mosque, or it is only prohibited to combine both acts at the same time, in the sense that if each is made separately, it will be permissible. If it is the former, it will be permissible to a menstruating woman to stay in the mosque in case of necessity, e.g. if she fears that someone may kill her should she does not enter the mosque, in severe cold weather, or when she finds no shelter other than the mosque. 'A'ishah said: The Prophet (peace be upon him) said to me: "Fetch me my cover from the mosque!" I said:

But I am menstruating. He replied: "Your menstruation is not in your hand."

Maimunah, the Prophet's wife, said: The Prophet (peace be upon him) was used to put his head in the lap of any of us, while she was menstruating, and would recite the Holy Qur'an. Any of us might spread the Prophet's cover for him in the mosque, while she was menstruating.

It was narrated by Abu Dawud on the authority of 'A'ishah that the Prophet (peace be upon him) said: "I do not permit one who is ritually impure due to seminal discharge or a menstruating woman to enter the mosque."

To reconcile between this hadith and the earlier ones, many scholars, such as Imam Al-Shafi'i, Imam Ahmad and others differentiated between the case of passing by the mosque and that of staying in the mosque. Some scholars forbade both passing by the mosque and staying in it by a menstruating woman, such as Imam Abu Hanifah and Imam Malik. Others did not forbade passing by the mosque, on the basis of the Qur'anic verse: **"...nor in a state of ceremonial impurity (except when travelling on the road), until after washing your whole body."** (4:43)

Imam Ahmad and others permitted the stay in the mosque for the sake of performing ablution. This opinion is supported   by the narration of 'Ata' bin Yasar, who said: I

saw men of the Prophet's Companions stay in the mosque
while they were ritually impure due to seminal discharge,
after performing ablution like that made before Prayer.

Perhaps this was because the mosque is most frequented
by the angles, who cannot enter a place where a ritually
impure person is present. For this reason the Prophet
(peace be upon him) forbade a ritually impure man to sleep
in the mosque. It was reported after 'A'ishah that she said:
If any of you has intercourse with his wife, he should not
sleep unless he performs ablution like that made before
Prayer. Who knows! He may die in his sleep. In another
hadith it was reported: ...because if he sleeps (while being
ritually impure) the angels will not attend his funeral.

The Prophet (peace be upon him) ordered one who was
ritually impure due to seminal discharge to perform
ablution before eating, drinking and in case he would
repeat intercourse with his wife. This is a proof that if one
who is ritually impure due to seminal discharge makes
ablution, the parts of ablution will become ritually pure,
which means that his state of ritual impurity will not be
complete.

However, if one has a minor impurity, or an impurity
lesser than major impurity, he will not be treated as one
who is ritually impure due to seminal discharge, in the
sense that the angels will not abstain from witnessing his
funeral, should he dies in his sleep, and that he will be
permitted to sleep and stay in the mosque.

This indicates that ritual impurity can be divided into parts, some of which may be removed from the parts of the body which are washed or wiped with the water of ablution. This is the opinion of the majority of scholars.

As regards a menstruating woman, whose impurity is continuous, is legally excused to stay, sleep and eat in the mosque, without making ablution. She is not forbidden to do what a ritually impure one is forbidden to do, in case of necessity.

On this basis, the preferable opinion of scholars is that a menstruating woman may recite the Holy Qur'an if she is in need of it. This is the opinion of Imam Malik, one of the two   opinions of Imam Al-Shafi'i and a narration after Imam Ahmad. This is in the case a menstruating woman is in need of reciting the Holy Qur'an, since she cannot make purification,   as is the case with one who is ritually impure due to seminal discharge, despite the fact the at her impurity is greater than the former, in the sense that she cannot   observe Fasting before the cessation of blood, while a ritually impure person can.

If it is argued that a menstruating woman is forbidden to observe Prayer before the cessation of blood, no matter she makes purification or not, and that her husband is prohibited to have intercourse with her, which entails more strict forbiddance on her part to enter the mosque or stay in it, this can be answered by the argument that a forbidden act may be permitted in case of necessity, such as the permission to drink blood and eat carrion and swine flesh in case of necessity.

Furthermore, some other acts which, though are less strictly prohibited, but cannot be permitted without necessity, such as wearing silk garments by men, drinking in gold or silver vessels, etc.

It is more strictly forbidden to pray to a direction other than the Qiblah, to pray with the private parts uncovered, or to pray while there is an impurity on one's body or garment. However, all of these may be permitted, or even become obligatory in case of necessity. Other less strictly prohibited acts cannot be permitted unless in case of necessity, such as recitation of the Holy Qur'an.

A ritually impure person due to a seminal discharge whose impurity is continuing because of his inability to make ritual washing or tayammum [dry ablution] shall be treated as the case of the menstruating woman mentioned previously, despite his occurs rarely.

The Prophet ordered menstruating women to get out on the occasion of `Ids and witness the celebration and good invocations made by people and pronounce takbir [Saying: Allahu Akbar (Allah is the Greatest)].

The Prophet also ordered menstruating and confined women to make Ihram, Talbyah, witness `Arafah while pronouncing remembrance of Allah and supplicating Him, throwing pebbles while remembering Allah, etc. All these are not disapproved for a menstruating or a confined woman, rather they are obliged to do that. A person who is ritually impure due to seminal discharge is discouraged to do these acts until he has a ritual washing, as he can this easily, which is not the case of a menstruating woman.

The forbiddance of a menstruating woman to circumambulate the Sacred House is justified with the cause of maintaining the sanctity of the mosque. Thus said some of the Hanafi scholars, as the school of Imam Abu Hanifah maintains that purification is an obligatory practice to be done before entering the mosque, but not an obligation that should be made inside it or a prerequisite to enter it. This justification has more in common with the saying that the circumambulation made without ablution is not prohibited. This is the opinion of Mansur bin Al-Mu'tamir and Hammad bin Abi Sulaiman, which was narrated after them by Imam Ahmad.

Abdullah said in his *Manasik*: I asked Shu'bah bin Hammad and Mansur about circumambulating the Sacred House without making ablution. They saw no harm in that. Abdullah said: I asked my father about that and he said: I prefer making ablution before circumambulation, since circumambulation is like Prayer.
There are two narrations after Imam Ahmad regarding the purification: whether it is a prerequisite of circumambulation or not. He also had to narrations regarding the necessity of purification during circumambulation.

Some Hanafi scholars maintained that purification is not obligatory before circumambulation, rather a supererogatory act. Neglecting purification, however, entails offering a sacrifice.

Those who argued that a person who has not made ablution can make circumambulation, may justify the forbiddance from circumambulation by maintaining the sanctity of the mosque, not because of circumambulation itself. During circumambulation it is permitted to talk, eat and drink, which is not the case with Prayer. The key of Prayer is purification, its sanctity begins soon after pronouncing the commencement takbir and ends with the pronouncement of taslim [saying As-salamu 'Alaikum wa rahmatul-lah (peace be upon you and Allah's Mercy and Blessings)]. Circumambulation does not resemble Prayer in the above-mentioned aspects.

It was said that people were forbidden to circumambulate the Sacred House while being nude, because of maintaining the sanctity of the mosque on one hand, and to avoid the sight of people on the other.
The proponents of this opinion said that the place of circumambulation is considered the most honorable places of Prayer, which cannot be void of pilgrims. Allah the Almighty said: "...**Wear your beautiful apparel at every time and place of Prayer...**" (7:31)

Thus a beautiful apparel should be worn when entering places of Prayer i.e. mosques. This is not the case with

Prayer itself, as a worshipper should cover his body for the purpose of Prayer, which may be performed at any place. If one performs Prayer individually in a dark house, he will be required to cover himself for the purpose of Prayer. As for circumambulation, it cannot be made unless in the Sacred House. I'tikaf also can be made in any mosque, but cannot be made elsewhere.

Based on the above, a menstruating woman and a person who is ritually impure due to seminal discharge are not prohibited to circumambulate the Sacred House, as it is not prohibited to make circumambulation without performing ablution, for they both are not prohibited to enter the mosque. If both are driven by a necessity to enter the mosque, they will be entitled to that right more than one who makes circumambulation without ablution, despite having no excuse to do that.

Consider the case of one who has not performed ablution, who is forbidden to perform Prayer or touch the Holy Qur'an, despite his ability to make purification. Consider also that these acts are permissible to a person who is ritually impure due to seminal discharge. If he cannot make ablution, he may perform Prayer without neither washing nor Tayammum, according to one of the two opinions made by scholars on that question. This is the famous opinion of the schools of Imam Al-Shafi'i and Imam Ahmad.

It was also reported that some of the Companions performed Prayer while being ritually impure due to seminal discharge, before the Qur'anic verse regarding Tayammum was revealed.

*   *   *

Forbidding a menstruating woman to observe Fasting in Ramadan

A menstruating woman is not required to fast during her menses. She may instead make up for the days she did not fast in a month other than Ramadan. A traveler and a sick person who, though are able to fast, are given concession to make up for missed days in a month other than Ramadan. A menstruating woman, thus, who is originally forbidden to observe Fasting is more entitled to abide by the forbiddance. She is required to make up for the missed days of Fasting for one month only. If she suffers *Istihadah* [continual vaginal bleeding,] she is permitted to observe Fasting.

Forbidding a menstruating woman to perform Prayer

Prayer is a recurrent obligation repeated five times daily. Menstruation hinders from performing Prayer. If it is argued that a menstruating woman may perform Prayer in case of necessity, thus menstruation will not be regarded as a hindrance of Prayer in all cases, it will be deduced that Fasting and circumambulation have sanctity more than Prayer, which is not correct, since Prayer is so sacred that it cannot be performed by a menstruating woman. The Prayer performed while woman is ritually pure is, thus, regarded a compensation of the Prayer missed while she was ritually impure.

Argument:

It is argued that if circumambulation if permitted during menstruation, both Prayer and Fasting will also be permitted during menstruation, which can never occur.

Refutation:

Fasting during menstruation is ultimately unnecessary, since the obligation of Fasting is limited to one month only, which can be made up for in any month, should one cannot observe Fasting in Ramadan. Since obligatory Fasting is prohibited during menstruation, supererogatory Fasting will be even prohibited. A menstruating woman has a good chance to make up for the missed days of Fasting whenever she becomes ritually pure, exactly as one who is forbidden to perform supererogatory Prayer in certain times, is also permitted to offer it in other certain times. Thus, such fasting cannot be permitted, as there is no compelling circumstances to observe it.

Supererogatory Prayer is not permitted at times when performing Prayer is disapproved, unless it is a causal Prayer i.e. that is performed for a certain need. The preferable opinion is that a causal Prayer is permitted at times of the disapproval of performing Prayer, since if it is delayed until the time of disapproval passes, it may miss its purpose.

For this reason, a woman who suffers from *Istihadah* [continual vaginal bleeding] is permitted to perform Prayer and observe Fasting, since she has a continuing excuse.

If Prayer is permitted during menstruation, it will not be a hindrance from Prayer in all cases, since menstruation is concurrent with all women. The Prophet (peace be upon him) said to 'A'ishah concerning menstruation: "Allah has prescribed it on the daughters of Adam." i.e. all females. If the Prophet permitted women to perform Prayer during menstruation, it will be equally permissible to perform it during menstruation and after purification.

Furthermore, if all acts of devotion are permitted during menstruation, it will not be a hindrance any more, though the ritual impurity due to seminal discharge and minor impurity, i.e. the state of being without ablution, are considered a hindrance, which entails a great contradiction. If all acts of devotion become prohibited during menstruation, except for Prayer, it will be an even greater contradiction.

Thus a menstruating woman is not permitted to perform Prayer, as she can do that after she becomes ritually pure, which is her predominant condition. She is permitted, however, to pronounce Talbyah, remembrance of Allah and supplication as much as she wishes.
A menstruating woman is ordered to wash herself, since the Prophet (peace be upon him) ordered Asma' to take a ritual bath upon making Ihram, when the former suffered puerperal bleeding following the birth of Muhammad bin Abu Bakr. He (peace be upon him) also ordered all women

o follow suit. He further ordered 'A'ishah, when she menstruated to take a bath and make Ihram for pilgrimage.

He (peace be upon him) also permitted menstruating women to pronounce Talbyah, attend 'Arafah, supplicate Allah and remember Him without a need to take a ritual bath or perform ablution. Contrary to persons who are ritually impure due to seminal discharge, all these acts will not be disapproved on their part of menstruating women. This is because they are in need to do that, and ritual bathing or ablution cannot remove their continuous ritual impurity. But this is not the case concerning the ritual bathing made before Ihram, for it is made for the sake of cleanliness, such as the bathing on Friday.
A question is raised here: Can Tayammum be a compensation of such kinds of bathing, as well as the washing of a deceased when water is lacking?

There are two opinions, one is for and the other is against.
The previously mentioned bathing i.e. which woman do even she is menstruating or confined, is not like ritual bathing made after ritual impurity due to seminal discharge, nor like ablution made to be out of the state of minor impurity. However, a menstruating woman is not required to take a bath upon her arrival to Mecca and at the occasion of attending 'Arafah.

As a menstruating woman is forbidden to perform Prayer, but not forbidden to say remembrance of Allah without disapproval, the difference becomes clear between when in needed and what is not needed.

Argument:

A ritually impure person due to seminal discharge and one who is not taking ablution are permitted to say all kinds of remembrance of Allah, thus there is no restriction is this.

Refutation:

A ritually impure person due to seminal discharge is forbidden to recite the Holy Qur'an. It is disapproved for him to make Adhan [call for Prayer,] deliver a sermon or to sleep without performing ablution. It is also disapproved for him to perform the rituals without purification, despite his ability to make purification.

It is also recommended to one who is not taking ablution to make purification before the remembrance of Allah. The Prophet (peace be upon him) said: "I did not like to remember Allah without being ritually pure." A menstruating woman, however, is not recommended to do any of these things. At the same time, the remembrance she makes without purification, is not disapproved, due to the uninterrupted reports in the Prophetic Sunnah which supported that.

*　　*

Recitation of the Holy Qur'an by a menstruating woman

Scholars disputed over this question. There is no proof from the Sunnah that forbids a menstruating woman to recite the Holy Qur'an. As for the hadith: "Neither a menstruating woman, nor that who becomes ritually impure due to seminal discharge is permitted to recite any portion from the Holy Qur'an," this narration is judged as weak by the scholars of hadith studies. It is not traced back to the Prophet (peace be upon him)

If recitation of the Holy Qur'an is prohibited to menstruating women, the Prophet (peace be upon him) would have prohibited women in his time and the judgment would have been conveyed to the Muslim community through the Mothers of Believers i.e. the Prophet's wives.

*   *

Menstruation and I`tikaf (Seclusion in a Mosque for worship)

This also indicates that prohibiting a menstruating woman to circumambulate is just like prohibiting her to seclude in the mosque because of its sacredness. Otherwise, menstruation does not invalidate her seclusion, because it is out of her hand. The mosque is prohibited for her and not seclusion, because she is not obliged to stay in the mosque. If it had been permissible for her in spite of continuous menstruation, the mosque would have been permissible for the menstruating women.

As for circumambulation, it is not to be performed except in the Sacred Mosque as it is restricted to a certain place

79

It is not like I`tikaf, for it is permissible for the person who secluded himself to get out of the mosque for necessities such as alleviating the call of nature and eating and drinking.

When he is out of the mosque, he is still in the state of seclusion, and it is not permissible for him to have intercourse with his wife as Allah said: "Do not associate with your wives while you are in retreat in the mosques." The phrase "in the mosques" is related to the phrase "in retreat" and not the verb "associate", because having intercourse with one's wife is not permissible in the mosque whether for a person who secluded himself in or not. When such person is obliged to get out of the mosque for necessity, it is not permissible for him to have intercourse with his wife.

As long as this act resembles I`tikaf, and it is permissible for a menstruating woman to get out for necessity, menstruation has not cut off her I`tikaf. Allah mentioned the acts of I`tikaf, circumambulation and prayer when He referred to cleaning and sanctifying His House as He said: **"Sanctify My House for those who compass it round, or use it as a retreat, or bow, or prostrate themselves (therein in Prayer)."**

Preventing menstruating women to enter the mosque is one of the signs of its purity and sanctity. Circumambulation is just like I`tikaf not prayer, because prayer could be performed in any part of the earth and is not restricted to a certain mosque. During prayer, certain acts are prohibited while during circumambulation or I`tikaf, they are not.

Summary

In fact, circumambulation is an act of devotion that is not related to Ihram. Therefore, obligatory circumambulation is only due after the first part of Hajj. The pilgrim is to circumambulate as Allah said: **"Then let them complete the rites prescribed for them, perform their vows, and (again) circumambulate the Ancient House."** Pilgrims circumambulate after they have finished the first part of Hajj and nothing is prohibited for them except having intercourse with their wives.

If a pilgrim has intercourse during this period, his Hajj is not nullified according to the unanimous agreement of Muslim scholars. If it has been an act of worship, it is restricted to the Sacred Mosque, but I`tikaf may be done in all mosques. Allah enjoined that his House be sanctified and purified for those who circumambulate, seclude themselves in it, bow and prostrate. circumambulation is not a type of prayer. When one does not perform any of the rituals required in Hajj or `Umrah, he should slaughter an animal (a sheep, goat or a camel).

If he does not perform an obligatory act during circumambulation, this is a point of discourse where scholars exert their efforts to reach a judgment.
Is it similar to the one who does not perform any of the rituals required in Hajj or `Umrah? Is this judgment applicable only in case of ignoring an independent ritual? Or ignoring it while he is able to do it? Or ignoring a ritual closely related to Hajj and `Umrah?

There are claims that when a women is unable to circumambulate because of menstruation, she should return home while she is still in her state of Ihram, treated just like those who are prevented from performing Hajj (Muhsar), Hajj is no longer obligatory on her, or the obligatory circumambulation is not due on her; all such claims do not conform with the fundamentals of Islamic legislation. I know none of the Imams who delivered such ruling as in this case.

As for the saying of some Imams that she should slaughter an animal or return home in her state of Ihram, this is a generalized saying only applicable on their age. In such age, a woman could stay in Mecca until menstruation is over and she can perform circumambulation accordingly.

The scholars of this age used to order those responsible for the Hajj journey to stay in Mecca until menstruating women are pure and they perform circumambulation.

Imam Malik and other scholars see that the person in charge of the Hajj journey should stay until menstruating women are pure and they perform circumambulation. Yet his followers say that he is not entitled to stay at this age because of the delay and harm that afflict him.

Scholars' stipulation that ritual purity is a condition for circumambulation should be interpreted that when a woman is able to circumambulate when she is ritually impure, and not when she is unable to do so. If some say that circumambulation is obligatory in both ritual purity and impurity, there is disagreement with such saying. Allah knows best. May Allah have peace on Prophet Muhammad.

Q: The Sheikh of Islam was asked about menstruation which happens to many women during Hajj and the various cases of it. Some may menstruate at the very beginning of Hajj while others during the Tashriq days?

- The first case: A woman may menstruate at the beginning of the month, and she can not circumambulate except in this case of ritual impurity. When standing at `Arafah, some yellowish and brownish materials get out of her vagina even after she has been pure. What is the legal judgment in this case?

- The second case: A woman usually menstruates from the fifth or the ninth till the seventeenth day of the month or even more. She stood at `Arafah, threw the pebbles, and performed the Ifadah circumambulation while she is menstruating. Besides, she has not managed to perform `Umrah.

- The third case: A woman stood at `Arafah, threw the pebbles, and headed for the Ifadah circumambulation but she menstruated. She has not performed it and concealed the matter. She had the desire to perform `Umrah but she did not. She returned home without circumambulation, performing `Umrah, or slaughtering an animal (as a ransom).

A: A menstruating woman should perform all rituals except for circumambulation according to the traditions of the Prophet (peace be upon him) and the unanimous agreement of Muslim Imams. The Prophet (peace be upon him) said: "A menstruating woman should perform all rituals except for circumambulation." When Asm`a bint Abi Bakr gave birth to a baby at Dhi Al-Hulaifah, the Prophet ordered her to wash and enter into the state of Ihram. When `A'ishah menstruated at Saraf, he ordered her to wash and enter into the state of Ihram for Hajj, stand at `Arafah, but she should not circumambulate around the Sacred House.

What if yellowish and brownish materials get out of her vagina? There are three opinions adopted by scholars in Ahmed's juristic school and others.

The first opinion is that such yellowish and brownish materials are signs of menstruation. The second is that they are not. The third is the most proper one. If such materials get out along with the black and red blood, they are a sign of menstruation. Otherwise they are not, because women used to send to `A'ishah a piece of cotton they have put in  their vaginas in order to check whether they become  pure  or not. `A'ishah used to reply: Do not haste until you see it white (without any other colored materials).

Thus before seeing it white, they used to consider all this period as the monthly period. Umm `Atiyah also said: After purity from menstruation, we were not used to pay the least attention to yellowish and brownish materials getting out of the vagina.

According to the unanimous agreement of Muslim scholars, ritual impurity is a condition for circumambulation around the House. In case of other rituals, impurity is not a condition. As for circumambulation between Safa and Marwah, there is dispute among scholars about it but the majority of them believe that ritual purity is not one of its conditions. As for the rest of rituals, ritual purity is not a condition according to the unanimous agreement of Muslim scholars.

There is dispute among scholars regarding ritual purity. Is it a condition for proper circumambulation just as for prayer?

Or is it an obligatory act which, if ignored, one should slaughter an animal? In this last case, it is similar to the one who enters into the state of Ihram from a place other than the Miqat or the one who did not throw the pebbles.

There are two famous points of view on this case as reported by Ahmed. The most famous one is also adopted by Malik and Shafi`i. It stipulates that ritual purity is a condition for circumambulation. If a person circumambulates in a state of ritual impurity or during menstruation whether he/she forgets or has not known so, but later knew, he should perform circumambulation again.

The second opinion is that ritual purity is obligatory and if one was impure, he should slaughter an animal. According to Abu Hanifah, the one in a state of major ritual impurity or a menstruating woman should slaughter a camel, while a person in a state of minor ritual impurity should slaughter a sheep.

As for Imam Ahmed, he did not define the type of animal to be slaughtered whether it is a camel or a sheep. He stated it clearly when he asked about a person in a state of major ritual impurity who circumambulated, and Imam Ahmed replied that he should slaughter an animal. Some of his followers apply these rulings when a person has an excuse such as forgetfulness, while others apply them as they are without making distinction whether a person is excused or not.

Scholars who stipulate ritual impurity for circumambulation argue that it is just like prayer. An-Nasa'i and others reported that Ibn `Abbas narrated that the Prophet (peace be upon him) said: "A naked person should not circumambulate around the Sacred House." Allah also said: **"Wear your beautiful apparel at every time and place of prayer."** This verse was revealed when the polytheists used to circumambulate around the Sacred House while they are naked except for a tribe called Al-Hums who used to wear their clothes during circumambulation.

Naked polytheists used to argue that they had disobeyed Allah in these clothes and hence they would pit them off during circumambulation. If they found clothes worn by Al-Hums tribe, they would wear them; otherwisde, they would circumambulate while they are naked. Once they circumambulate in Al-Hums clothes, they would throw them away.

These were innovations made by the polytheists during circumambulation and they also prohibited some kinds of foods when they are in a state of Ihram. Therefore Allah revealed this verse: **"Wear your beautiful apparel at every time and place of prayer: eat and drink: but waste not be excess, for Allah loves not the wasters. Say: who has forbidden the beautiful (gifts) of Allah, which He has produced for his servants, and the things, clean and pure, (which He has provided) for sustenance?"** He also said: **"When they do aught that is**

shameful, they say: "We found our fathers doing so": and "Allah commanded us thus;" say: "Nay, Allah never commands what is shameful: do you say of Allah what you know not?"

The shameful act mentioned in the verse is circumambulation around the Sacred House while they are naked.

Hence, major ritual impurity is obligatory for circumambulation according to the unanimous agreement of Muslim scholars and the divine texts. As for considering it as a condition for circumambulation just like prayer, there is dispute among scholars in this regard. Scholars who adopt that it is not a condition believe that there are obligatory acts in the Hajj ransomed by slaughtering an animal. Such acts are not conditions for a sound Hajj and if a pilgrim did not perform them on purpose or forgetfully, he should slaughter an animal. This is not the case with prayer.

Are there obligatory acts in prayer which, if not done, it is still valid? Is it not valid if he did not perform them forgetfully? There is a famous dispute on this point. Abu Hanifah believes that there are obligatory acts such as reciting surah Al-Fatihah and tranquility. If such acts were not done, prayer is still valid. This is one of the opinions in Ahmed's juristic school. According to Ahmed, congregational prayer is obligatory but it is not a condition for the validity of prayer. When a person does not perform some acts forgetfully, and he prostrated twice after the end of prayer, such act is obligatory in prayer. Yet there are other acts such as avoiding impurities which, if ignored, a person must perform the prayer again within the legal time. If such time is over, he should not perform it again.

As for the second question:

When a woman menstruates and becomes pure before the Slaughter Day, she is not entitled to perform the arrival circumambulation. She is to perform the Ifadah circumambulation on the Slaughter Day or after it. If she perform the Ifadah circumambulation while she is ritually pure, but later she menstruates and has not become pure before leaving Mecca, she is not entitled to perform the Farewell circumambulation according to the tradition of Prophet (peace be upon him). He allowed for the woman who circumambulated during her purity, but later menstruated not to perform the Farewell Circumambulation. When his wife, Mother of the Believers Safiah menstruated on the Slaughter Day, he said: "Will she prevent us from leaving Mecca?" They replied: "She has already performed the Ifadah circumambulation." He said: "She is not entitled to perform the Farewell circumambulation."

If she menstruated before Ifadah, she must stay in Mecca until she is ritually pure and then she can circumambulate. People with her should stay as well if they can. In old times, roads were secure and people used to visit Mecca throughout the whole year. A woman, her family and those responsible for the Hajj journey were able to stay in Mecca until she is ritually pure and performs circumambulation. Scholars used to order people to do so.

They may even ordered those in charge of the Hajj journey to stay until menstruating women are pure as did the Prophet (peace be upon him).

Abu Hurairah (may Allah be pleased with him) said: A person may act as a prince while he is not. It is a woman who menstruated before Ifadah and the people her would stay until she is ritually pure and performs circumambulation.

Nowadays, most women could not stay after the Hajj party leaves Mecca. They usually leave Mecca a day, two or three after the Tashriq. A woman may have menstruated on the Slaughter Day and she will be pure after seven days or more. She could not stay in Mecca until she is ritually pure, either because she does not have enough money or there are no people to stay with them and return home in their company.

She may be afraid that a harm may afflict her, her money may be spent during such stay, or she may return home after her company. Besides, the party in her company may not be able to stay with her either because they can not return alone, or because they fear that they may be exposed to any danger that affects their lives and money. Sometimes, they may be able to stay, but they do not do it. Thus her excuse remains the same.

This is a very common matter. Once this woman circumambulated while she is menstruating and later ransomed this act by slaughtering a camel or a sheep, her Hajj is sound according to Abu Hanifah and Ahmed who believe that major ritual impurity is not a condition for circumambulation. Besides, she has an excuse. Yet, is it permissible for her to circumambulate while she has an excuse? This is a controversial point among scholars. In addition, if circumambulation is considered as a condition of Hajj, can one perform Hajj without taking this condition into consideration? Is circumambulation valid in this case? This the point most people need to know. It is more convenient to say that a person is entitled to perform the obligatory acts he could do.

As for acts which he can not do, they are not obligatory. In this case, a woman will circumambulate, wash even if she had been menstruating as when she enters into the state of Ihram, puts pieces of cloth or the like around her private parts. This is the most reasonable legal opinion for the following reasons:

First: this woman can do nothing except for any of the following five acts.

1. She should stay until she is ritually pure and then circumambulates. What will be the case if she has no money to support her or a place to take as shelter? If she did not return home and stayed in Mecca, some may oblige her to adultery or even rob her money if she has any.

2. She should return home without performing circumambulation and she stays there in her state of Ihram until she is able to return to Mecca once again. If she can not, she should be in her state of Ihram until

she dies.

3. She should get out of the state of Ihram just like those
   prevented from completing Hajj, but she is still entitled
   to complete it once she enters Mecca according to the
   unanimous agreement of Muslim scholars. This same
   case applies to those prevented from completing the
   Hajj. Yet, if they enter into the state of Ihram with the
   intention of performing Hajj or `Umrah, and later they
   were prevented from completing it, are they entitled to
   perform it again? In this regard, there are two famous
   opinions adopted by Ahmed. The first of them, also
   adopted by Malik and Shafi`I, is that they should not
   perform it again. The second, also adopted by Abu
   Hanifah, is that they should.

Both parties mentioned the Case `Umrah. Some say that
the Prophet (peace be upon him) performed it again while
others say that he did not. His companions were more than
one thousand and four hundreds, and those who performed
 Umrah with him next year were much less in number. It
was called the Case `Umrah because there was some sort
of a case between the Prophet (peace be upon him) and the
polytheists, not because he performed it again. It was an
independent `Umrah.

4. Whenever a woman expects to menstruate and hence
   she can not circumambulate while she is pure, she is
   not to be enjoined to perform Hajj. About fifty percent
   of women menstruate either on the tenth day of the
   month or days before it. Their menstruation lasts one,

two or three days after the Tashriq. Therefore, they, almost always, can not perform the Ifadah Circumambulation when they are ritually pure. Even if a woman performed Hajj, she must have recourse to any of the above-mentioned three options, unless she would circumambulate while she is menstruating.

It is well known that a woman is not to be enjoined to perform the first option, because it leads to doing away with her religion and worldly affairs. It is also well known that Allah prohibits such matters, how comes that He enjoins it?

The second option is not also permissible for the following three reasons:

First: Allah never orders anybody to stay in the state of Ihram until he dies. When a person is prevented from completing rituals by an enemy, he has the full right to end the state of Ihram according to the unanimous agreement of Muslim scholars. If he had been prevented because of an illness or poverty, this is a famous point of dispute among scholars. There is no objection to those who allowed him to end the state of Ihram.

Those who prevented him from ending the state of Ihram say that the harm caused by illness or poverty does not come to an end once he put an end to the state of Ihram. In case of prevention by an enemy, putting an end to the state of Ihram will allow him to return to his country and do whatever acts prohibited during Ihram. If he lost Hajj, he can put an end to the state of Ihram by performing a compensatory `Umrah.

As for the sick, once he restores his health, he can resume his Hajj or `Umrah. The poor person's need to complete the Hajj journey is just like his need to return, and therefore both the sick and the poor should not put an end to the state of Ihram. They will not make use of ending it. If this argument is valid, preventing him from putting an end to the state of Ihram is the most proper opinion. Otherwise, the first opinion that he should put an end to the state of Ihram is more proper. If the second opinion is adopted, this means that there must be agreement among scholars that once the state of Ihram may cause any harm, it is permissible for one to put an end to it.

It is well known that if the woman keeps her state of Ihram, it is prohibited to have sexual intercourse with her. In another juristic school, even the introductory acts of intercourse are prohibited. It is also prohibited for her to marry, apply perfumes and shooting according to the opinion of some scholars. Yet, our religion never enjoins such.

If some claim that a person prevented from completing Hajj or `Umrah because of severe illness or abject poverty which does not allow him to travel, and hence he keeps his state of Ihram, such saying is refuted according to the fundamentals of religion. No jurist has ever said that a very sick person should keep his state of Ihram until he dies. Instead, another one is to perform Hajj on behalf of him if he has sufficient money according to Shafi`I and Ahmed.

According to Imam Malik, physical ability makes Haj obligatory on a Muslim. According to Abu Hanifah, both physical and financial abilities are required for Hajj. Ahmed shares this point of view. None of the Muslim Imams ever said that a very sick person is allowed to perform Hajj or `Umrah. How comes that he keeps the state of Ihram until he dies and is entitled to complete Hajj?

Second: Such woman may return home and then travel to Mecca once again but she may be exposed to the very same conditions of the first journey. She can not return home except with her company and she may menstruate during her stay at Mecca.

Third: This means that such woman will travel twice for Hajj without doing anything illegal. This ruling is not in conformity with the fundamentals of religion. Allah made Hajj obligatory on people just once during their lifetime. A person may perform Hajj again because he committed an illegal act that invalidated his Ihram.

Yet, such person does so because he did not conform with the regular procedures of Hajj such as not standing at `Arafah. He may have no idea about the road, or followed another which is not tracked by most people, and hence he did not perform Hajj and he should perform it again. A menstruating woman has not made anything in disconformity with the rules of Hajj. Therefore, the Prophet (peace be upon him) allowed her not to perform the Farewell and Arrival circumambulation as in the traditions narrated by `A'ishah and Safiah.

As for the second option that she should put an end to the state of Ihram just like the people prevented from completing Hajj or `Umrah, this is a more proper argument as said by some scholars. Her fear to stay in Mecca until she circumambulates is similar to her fear of an enemy who prevents her from circumambulation. A Muslim is never enjoined to perform Hajj while there are conditions that may prevent him from doing it. If a person believes that if he intends to perform Hajj, but he will be prevented from completing it, Hajj is not obligatory on him at all. Safe roads to Mecca and enough time to travel are obligatory conditions according to the unanimous agreement of Muslims.

There is dispute whether these conditions necessitate Hajj i.e. when a man has enough money and the means of transport but he fears that the way to Mecca may not be safe or there is not enough time to go there, is Hajj obligatory on him? Can anyone perform Hajj on behalf of him after he dies? Or is it not obligatory on him at all? There are two opinions in this regard.

If a scholar says that such woman is prevented from completing Hajj and hence she can end the state of Ihram, he is entitled to adopt the first option that Hajj is not obligatory or even desirable for women. According to such argument, Hajj is not legal for most women during these times because they are not able to perform some obligatory acts during circumambulation.

It is well know that this later opinion does not conform with the fundamentals of religion. When one is unable to perform some of the obligatory or desirable acts of worship, he should perform the acts he is able to do. The Prophet (peace be upon him) said: "If I commanded you to do something, do whatever you can (of it)." Allah also said: **"So fear Allah as much as you can."**

It is also well known that prayer and other acts of worship greater than circumambulation are obligatory even if one can not perform some of its conditions and prerequisites. How comes that Hajj is not obligatory once a person is unable to perform some of its conditions and prerequisites?

Likewise, some may say that she should not perform the Ifadah circumambulation. This is also in disconformity with the fundamentals of religion. Hajj is just standing at `Arafah and circumambulation with the latter being the best of the two pillars. Therefore, it is to be performed whether in Hajj, `Umrah, or even alone. There are certain conditions for circumambulation which are not required for standing at `Arafah. How comes that Hajj is permissible without circumambulation?

It is more suitable to say that it is permissible for her to perform the Ifadah circumambulation before standing at `Arafah. In this case, it is permissible for her to circumambulate before or after standing at `Arafah. Yet, none of the Muslim Imams has permitted such act. There is an exception reported by the people of Basra who narrated that Imam Malik sees that it is permissible to circumambulate before standing at `Arafah if one has done so forgetfully or out of ignorance and later returned home. In this case, he is not entitled to perform the Ifadah circumambulation.

Therefore, it may be said that the same case is permissible for a menstruating woman if she has not managed to circumambulate before standing at `Arafah. Yet, I know none of the Imams who professed such opinion.

As for the case reported by Malik, one may say that when a person forgets to circumambulate or even does not know that it is obligatory, his return to perform Hajj against is a great burden. Therefore, the order is not required for such excuse. The same thing is applicable as far as ritual purity is concerned according to Ahmed's juristic school. If a person circumambulated while he is in a state of ritual impurity, but he forgot so, he has an excuse and therefore, he may slaughter an animal.

If he managed to perform most obligatory acts, how comes that Hajj is not due while he has not done just some acts? It should be known that a menstruating woman circumambulation is permissible and she should slaughter an animal.

As for performing the obligatory circumambulation first before standing at `Arafah, it is not permissible at all. If one forgets, the order of performing acts of worship is not necessary according to the unanimous agreement of Muslim scholars. Yet, if one is unable, the order is necessary as in the prerequisites of prayer. The same thing applies when one has no enough time to perform such acts according to the agreement of the majority of Muslim scholars.

If   a   post-menstruating   woman   has   the   ability   to circumambulate before standing at `Arafah  when she is ritually  pure,  and  after standing at `Arafah but when she ritually   impure,   she   should   not circumambulate except after standing at `Arafah. From this very perspective, it is not allowed for a woman to fast before the advent of Ramadan because she menstruates at Ramadan. Yet, she fasts once its time is obligatory.

According   to   the   unanimous   agreement   of   Muslim scholars, if there is contradiction between the time of a certain act of worship and some of its conditions and prerequisites,   ignoring   some   of   the   latter   is   more acceptable. If a person has the ability to pray before time is due with complete ritual purity and to avoid all sorts of impurities, while he can not do the same when its time is due, it is not permissible for him to perform it before its due time according to the Qur'an, Sunnah and the unanimous agreement of Muslim scholars. He should perform it at its due time.

Similarly acts of worship are not to be delayed after their time is due. Instead, they should be done on time as far as possible. Yet, if one has an excuse, it is permissible for him to perform tow prayers together. There are tow appointed times for prayer; one for ordinary people and the other is for those who have an excuse. When a person performs two prayers together at the same time, he performed them at their due legal time. He has not missed any of them neither he did any before its time is due according to the unanimous agreement of Muslim scholars.

The same rule is applicable to standing at `Arafah. If one stood before or after  its time is due, it is not permissible according to the unanimous agreement of Muslim scholars. Ifadah circumambulation is to be done  after standing at `Arafah on the Day of Slaughter and the following days. Is it permissible to circumambulate after midnight on the night of Slaughter? This is a controversial point among scholars.

Once these four cases are invalid, there remains the fifth:

She should do what she can and let aside what she can not. This opinion is supported by the divine texts which handle this matter and it is not contradictory with any of the fundamentals of religion.

Divine texts indicate that ritual purity is obligatory as the Prophet (peace be upon him) said: "A menstruating woman is to perform all rituals except for circumambulating around the Sacred House." This indicates that the command here is obligatory as he said: "When any of you passes urine, feces or the like, he should not perform prayers unless he performed ablution."

He also said: "Allah will not accept your prayer unless you performed ablution." He also said: "Allah will not accept the prayer of a major woman unless she wore a veil." He also advised a woman saying: "Clean it (your dress) well, wash it and then pray while wearing it." He also said: "A naked person should not circumambulate around the Sacred House." All these are obligatory on the condition that one is able to perform them as Allah said: **"So fear Allah as much as you can."** The Prophet (peace be upon him) also said: "If I commanded you to do something, do whatever you can (of it)."

Now it turns out that she can not stay at Mecca while she is unable because she harbors fears for herself, her religion and money. She is not to be ordered to continue in her state of Ihram, return home and travel to Mecca again although she does not have the ability to do so and the same thing may happen again without the least sin on her part. Putting an end to the state of Ihram is not permissible and the obligatory act of circumambulation is still to be done. Circumambulation is almost similar to prayer.

There is no proof that circumambulation is not accepted if performed by a person in a state of major ritual impurity. Yet, there are proofs that ritual purity is obligatory.

Hence, there is disagreement among scholars whether ritual purity is a condition or just an obligatory act. Such disagreement did not occur as far as prayer is concerned.

The second proof is that ritual purity is a condition for circumambulation. It is well known that ritual purity is required more in prayer than in circumambulation and that it is like veiling one's `aurah  and  avoiding impurities. Veiling  `aurah is required more in circumambulation than in prayer, because it is obligatory during and after circumambulation because doing it while one is naked is an act of the polytheists which the Prophet (peace be upon him) generally prohibited. It is permissible for a post-menstruating woman to circumambulate and pray according to the unanimous agreement of Muslims. Her impurity is similar to others but she has an excuse.

As long as the conditions for prayer are not to be fulfilled once a person is unable to do them, the same thing applies more to circumambulation. In case of necessities, a person may pray when he is naked or in a state of minor and major ritual impurity. He may perform tayammum (dry ablution) and pray even if he had been in a state of major ritual impurity.

If he is unable to perform ablution or tayammum, it is permissible for him to pray without each according to the agreement of the majority of Muslim scholars. But a menstruating woman is not to pray, because prayer is not obligatory on her. Prayer is repeated every and each day, and her prayer during such days stands for prayer during menstruation. Therefore, she is enjoined to re-fast and not to re-perform the prayers she missed during menstruation. Fasting is observed in just one month throughout the year.

If she is not able to fast during Ramadan while she is in a state of ritual purity, she should fast in any other month. She is not to do the same, but fasting is moved to another month.   If she is unable to fast continuously because of old age or severe illness, she is not required to fast. Yet she should compensate for it by feeding a needy on each day according to the majority of Muslim scholars such as Shafi`I, Abu Hanifah and Ahmed. According to Malik, she is not to feed anyone.

As for prayer, it is impossible for anyone not to perform any of its acts. He should do what he can. If he is unable to perform all actions made by the head and the body, he is not required to do them according to Abu Hanifah, Ahmed in a narration and Malik in one of the narrations. The other opinion is that he should nod with his eyes and have in mind the actions performed during prayer. This is the opinion of Shafi`I and Ahmed in another narration. The first opinion is rather closely related to divine texts and intellectual meditation.

As for Hajj, she can only perform it according to the mentioned procedure. If she can do just this, that is what she can do. This is similar if one can not circumambulate except when riding or when he is in a state of major ritual impurity.

*　　*　　*

Here, two questions may arise:

First: Would you consider the menstruating woman just like those unable to enter Mecca? If she wants to perform Hajj and has the ability to circumambulate, it is OK. If she can not, she could authorize a person to do it on behalf of her.

Second: If the Legislator has not made it legal for her to pray during menstruation, while a person in a state of major ritual impurity or a post-menstruating may perform dry ablution, it is clear that no act of worship is to be performed during menstruation.

As for the first question, once she managed to enter Mecca but she can not perform some obligatory acts, Hajj is still obligatory on her according to the unanimous agreement of Muslim scholars. The same case is applicable when one enters Mecca but is unable to avoid impurities. He must perform Hajj, but he is not entitled to stick to complete ritual purity. It is also applicable when one can not circumambulate except while riding or when he is carried or when he is unable to throw the pebbles. In such case, he may authorize a person to perform such acts on behalf of him.

*   *

The prayer of a menstruating woman

A menstruating women does not to pray, because her former prayers may compensate for those required during the monthly period. If she becomes pure but still some blood gets out of her vagina, she should pray, even if such blood may cause impurity and hence invalidated her prayer.

Yet, she is to be excused because of such blood. Allah distinguished between those who excuse and those who have not. Therefore, if blood ceased and she can perform ablution and prayer, she must do so. Prayer is permissible even though blood may get out after the monthly period out of necessity.

Some may argue that prayer should not be performed by such woman or by a person in state of major ritual impurity (in case he has not found water to wash) just like a woman in her monthly period. As long as Allah ordered post-menstruating women to pray, one comes to know that menstruation does not conform with prayer at all. It does not conform with circumambulation which resembles prayer.

In reply to this, one would say that a person in a major ritual impurity is just like a menstruating woman whose blood ceased and he can perform dry ablution (because no water is available). As for a post-menstruating woman, if she is not to pray during such the post-menstruation period, this means that she should not pray forever because her excuse happens very often.

Therefore, obligatory ritual purity is not fully required on her part. This indicates that if one can not perform a certain act of worship except by committing a prohibited action, it is rather better to perform it not to ignore it. The fundamentals of religion conform with this opinion. When a person in a major ritual impurity finds neither water nor dust for ablution, he should pray as well according to the majority of Muslim scholars because he is unable to perform ablution.

On the other side, menstruation fully contradicts with prayer. As for Hajj and circumambulation, one is required to perform it once during his lifetime, and it is not repeated many times just like prayer. If Hajj is not valid when one is excused in not doing a certain act, this means that Hajj will never be valid. The fundamentals of religion indicate that if one can not perform a certain act of worship because of an excuse, it is rather better to perform it not to ignore it.

It has been proven that during prayer, a menstruating woman has no excuse because prayer is an oft-repeated act of worship. In case of circumambulation, if she can not perform it except when she is menstruating, it is permissible because she is unable to perform it except in this way.

Third: One may say that this is a type of ritual purity which is not obligatory once a person is unable to perform just like the other types of ritual purities. If she had been post-menstruating and can not circumambulate except in such case, it is permissible for her according to the unanimous agreement of Muslim scholars. Whether ablution is obligatory or not in this case, this is a controversial point among scholars. She can even pray in this state although there may be some impurities. The same thing applies to a person in a minor or major ritual impurity who can find neither water nor dust. In this case, he can pray and circumambulate according to the most proper opinion of Muslim scholars.

Fourth: This is one of the conditions of circumambulation which is not   due because of the inability to do it just like any   other conditions. If he can not circumambulate except when he is naked, circumambulation while naked is much easier than prayer in the very same state according to the unanimous agreement of Muslim   scholars. Therefore, if one   can not circumambulate except when he is naked, it is permissible.

Scholars did not discuss this matter because it is very rare. It is almost impossible not to find clothes in Mecca. Yet, suppose that one's clothes are stolen and his company are leaving while he can not   lag behind them, he should do what he can in this case i.e. to circumambulate while he is naked.   In this case, he resembles a post-menstruating woman and the person who passes urine unintentionally because of an illness, although the prohibition to circumambulate when one is naked is known more to people than circumambulation during menstruation.

What   I have previously mentioned conforms with the generalized divine texts which handle this affair. It also conform with analogy to these fundamentals. The person who objects to my judgment may do so because he has not found any previous statement about this matter recorded by the followed Imams just like they have not discussed the possibility of circumambulation when one is naked because it never occurred during their times. Hence, they were not required to deliver a ruling on a matter which did not come in their mind. Their speech on this matter is very generalized because it was very rare or even non-existent. Their followers only mentioned such speech.

Therefore, Imam Malik made it obligatory on the person in charge of the Hajj journey to stay in Mecca until she is pure and circumambulates provided that the roads are safe and secure and no harm will afflict him if he did so.

During the era of the Companions, the person in charge of the Hajj journey used to stay in Mecca until menstruating women are pure and they circumambulated around the House. The late Maliki jurists believed that the Farewell circumambulation is not obligatory on the person in charge of the Hajj journey. Likewise, spending the night at Muzdalifah is not obligatory on those responsible for taking care of the pilgrims and providing them with water because they are unable to do it.

On the same footing, a menstruating woman is unable to circumambulate and hence its company used to stay in Mecca until she is pure. Scholars who believe that ritual purity is obligatory and not a condition for circumambulation should also say that in this case, ritual purity is not obligatory because of the inability to perform it. They say that when a person circumambulates while he is in a state of minor or major ritual impurity and he left Mecca, he should not return to circumambulate again because of the resultant hardships shouldered on him. How comes that ritual purity is obligatory on this woman although the hardships she will face are much more difficult?

Yet, some scholars say that this woman should slaughter an animal because she is not ritually pure during circumambulation. In this case, it is rather better to say that she should not slaughter an animal, because if one did not perform an obligatory act without the least negligence on his part, he is not be blamed. If he did not perform it out of forgetfulness or ignorance, this is another issue. It may be argued that she should slaughter an animal because such case is very rare.

There are similar cases as well. If an enemy prevented a person from throwing the pebbles and he was not able to do so until he returns to Mecca, or prevents him from standing at `Arafah until the night, or from performing the Farewell circumambulation, he is not be blamed at all.

The Prophet (peace be upon him) did not make the Farewell circumambulation obligatory on menstruating women. If a scholar said that ritual purity is a pillar and condition for circumambulation, it is not more important than prayer. It well known that the conditions of prayer are not due because of the inability to do them. It is much more suitable to apply this rule on the conditions of circumambulation.

This is my opinion in this issue. But for the people's dire

need for it, I would have never talked about it, because I have not found any scholar who handled this matter. Exerting one's efforts to reach a legal ruling in case of necessity is commanded by Allah. If I had reached a right ruling, it is the very same judgment of Allah and His Messenger, and all praise be to Allah. If it is wrong, it is my own and Satan insinuated it to me, and Allah and His Messenger are not responsible for it, even if I am absolved because of such error. Allah knows best. All praise be to Allah alone. May Allah have peace on Muhammad and his family.

Q: A woman menstruated before the Ifadah circumambulation and she has not become pure till the pilgrims' departure. She can not stay alone until she is pure. Is it permissible for her to circumambulate in this state out of necessity?
If it is permissible, is she entitled to slaughter an animal?
Is it desirable for her to wash herself before circumambulation? When a woman knows that she will not be pure until the pilgrims' departure and she can not stay after that, is Hajj still obligatory on her?
If it is not, is it desirable for her to perform circumambulation? Please tell us about the relevant ruling, may Allah grant you the nest reward.

A: All praise be to Allah. There are two famous opinions for scholars regarding ritual purity whether it is a condition of sound circumambulation.
First: It is a condition according to Malik, Shafi`I and

Ahmed in a narration.

Second: It is not a condition according to Abu Hanifah and Ahmed in the other narration.

According to the latter's opinion, if one circumambulated while he is in a state of minor or major ritual impurity or while there are impurities on his body, his circumambulation is valid but he should slaughter an animal.

Yet, there is disagreement among Ahmed's followers whether this is a general rule applicable to whoever forgets that he is ritually impure or not. Abu Hanifah believes that such animal is a camel if the woman was menstruating or in a state of major ritual impurity. When a woman can not circumambulate except when she is menstruating, it is permissible for her to do so, because Hajj is obligatory on her. No scholar has ever said that a menstruating woman is not entitled to perform it. It is not legal that obligatory acts become undue once a person is unable to perform some of them just like when a person is unable to perform ablution for prayer.

From Endowment to Marriage

Is it permissible to build a second floor over a Mihrab (altar)?

Q: An inquiry was made concerning building a second floor over a Mihrab to accommodate the Imam or anyone who takes care of the place, provided that no harm may be incurred because of such building?

A: It is permissible to build a second floor over the Mihrab that is built for purposes other than observing the five daily prayers. As for the mosque in which the regular five prayers are observed, there is a difference among jurists concerning building a second floor on it.

*   *

Assigning a will or an endowment for one's neighbors

Q: What is the judgment if a person assigns a will or an endowment for his neighbors without specifying any of them?

A: If no certain persons are specified by the term "neighbors", nor the deceased had a custom to call certain persons as his "neighbors" the juristic definition, which states that one's neighbors include forty houses to his right and forty to his left, is to be applied. The Prophet (peace be upon him) said: "The neighbors are forty from hither (the right side) and forty from thither (the left side). By whom in Whose Hand is my soul, none of you will have a perfect faith unless his neighbor is safe from his mischieves." Allah knows best.

*   *   *

The unmarried reciter

Q: What is the judgment of one who makes a graveyard as an endowment on the condition that an unmarried reciter of the Holy Qur'an be appointed for it. Can this endowment be effective, even when the reciter is married?

A: This condition is null and void. An unmarried man is even more worthy to this appointment than the single person, should they are equally qualified. The condition of being single does not serve a legal purpose here.

*   *   *

Is it permissible to privilege some of the children with a portion of the estate to the exclusion of others? Is it permissible to give to relatives from the estate

Q: A man assigned an endowment for a certain number of women, widows and orphans and conditioned that he should administer the affairs of such endowment in his lifetime, and that one of his eligible children, male or female, should succeed him after his death. As some of the children of the owner of the endowment are needy, the administrator of the endowment wants to privilege those needy children by giving them greater portion than the rest. Is this permissible?

A: If all the beneficiaries of an endowment is equally needy, preference is given to the relatives of the owner of the endowment. The Prophet said: "The (reward of) charity you give to Muslims is (only the reward of) a charity. However, the (reward of) charity that you give to your relatives is (the reward of) charity and maintaining of the ties of kinship." Thus there is a Prophetic command, either compulsory or recommendatory, that one should bequeath for some of his relatives who are not entitled to inherit him.

*

A woman dwelling next door to a group of men and a man dwelling next door to a group or women

Q: An accommodation is assigned for a group of ten poor persons. This accommodation includes an upstairs room inhabited by a single woman, for whom the owner of the endowment did not assign a place in it. She is not a relative of the deceased either. There is a main gate that by closing which both the accommodation and the upstairs room are not seen. Is it permissible that such woman live in the neighborhood of these poor people?

A: If the owner of the endowment assigned it for married or unmarried men only, she should not be admitted to it, in order to fulfill the condition of the donator. In all cases, single women are not permitted to dwell in the neighborhood of men and vise versa, in accordance to the precepts of Islamic Shari'ah. Allah knows best.

*

Assigning an endowment for the needy relatives of the deceased

Q: A woman assigned an endowment that should be distributed among the reciters of Qur'an on her grave. What remains should be spent on the poor, or for other charitable purposes. She had a maternal uncle who became bankrupt and could work no more. The administrator of the endowment refused to pay him a sum to support him for living. Is it permissible to oblige the administrator to give the deceased's uncle preference to others with regard to the right to receive money for his living?

A: The needy relatives of the deceased are more rightful to his endowment than any other equally needy persons.

Assigning the revenue of endowments for shrouding the poor deceased

Q: An endowment, which accrues annual revenues, is assigned for covering the expenses of shrouding the poor deceased. Is it permissible to spend the revenue in charity? Are the poor relatives of the owner of the endowment entitled to it?

A: If there is a surplus after covering the expenses of shrouds, the surplus should be spent for the interests of Muslims. If there are poor relatives of the donor, they are more rightful to it than others. Allah knows best.

*   *   *

Gift and gratuity
Charity and present

Q: Which is better, a charity or a present?

A: To start with, a charity is what is given for the sake of Allah to nonspecific persons and for no certain worldly purpose.

As for a present, it is given to honor some person therewith, either due to a cordial relation, friendship or in order to attain a certain interest.

The Prophet (peace be upon him) used to accept presents and give presents in return for them, in order to be free from indebtedness to others. He did not accept charity, which is a means of purifying the properties of people and themselves from sins. For this, as well as other reasons, the Prophet (peace be upon him) did not accept charity.

Based on this, charity is better, except when present is preferred for a certain reason, such as the case when the present is given to the Prophet (peace be upon him) in his life. The present is also preferred if given to a relative as a means of strengthening the ties of kinship, or to a fellow Muslim. In such instances a present may be better than a charity.

* * *

The Undefined Gift

Q: Is it permissible to assign an undefined thing as a gift, such as the case when a person offers the next year's fruits of a tree to a person as a gift? Can the former return in his gift?

A: The scholars differed over the undefined gift. Imam Malik claimed that it is permissible. He even made it permissible that one may grant something that he will inherit later on to another, without knowing its amount. He further claimed that it is permissible that one grants a portion of a house to another without telling him the area of such portion. According to Imam Malik, it is also permissible to grant something not found yet at the time of giving the grant, such as granting fruits that will grow later on at the current year or during the coming ten years.

Al-Shafi'i, on the other hand, did not approve of this, nor   did Abu Hanifah and Ahmad, according to the famous opinions of their schools.

However, Imam Ahmad, as well as Abu Hanifah, and others are not as strict as Imam Al-Shafi'i as regards making an undefined thing the subject of a settlement contract or absolution of it, should a person had already taken upon himself to give such undefined thing as a grant.

The Shafi'i necessitates that the subject of all contracts should be well defined, even in the case of Khul', dower, and the Jiziah. Most of scholars resort to a rather elastic approach regarding this respect. However, the preferred view is that of Imam Malik.

This question is related to another argument also, that is the exchange contracts, such as sale and marriage, which are binding, even before receiving the return. Receiving the return, which is the cause of the contract, is not a condition for making the contract binding.
Donations are like gifts and borrowed items.
Imam Abu Hanifah and Imam Al-Shafi'i viewed that the contract is not binding unless the return is received. As for Imam Malik, he was of the opinion that the contract becomes binding upon its conclusion.

Two narrations were related concerning Imam Ahmad's opinion of this. There is a disagreement in his school over this issue, similar to that raised in the case of a defined grant, whether the contract is binding upon its conclusion, or it is necessary to receive the return. Likewise, similar difference occurred concerning some instances of the borrowed items.

The Salaf Salih [the Righteous Ancestors] kept on lending the fruits of trees which were not ripe yet, offering the milk which was not milked yet and deemed that necessary.

Thus this kind of gift resembles the borrowed items, as the intent of the contract is to attain benefit. Therefore, this is the right of the person donated to, just like usufructs. It is valid to deal with a part of this contract such as the case with Musaqah.

As for the validity of such contract, it is unanimously agreed upon by scholars, whether it is existent or nonexistent, defined or undefined.

But a grant will not be considered a binding contract by those who deem the lending as a binding contract, such as Imam Abu Hanifah and Imam Al-Shafi'i. As for Imam Malik, he held that such contract is binding if it happens to include a condition or a prevailing custom. Imam Ahmad's opinion is marked by much disagreements and more elaboration.

A Woman Giving a Book to Her Husband as a Gift

Q: Can the brothers of a woman whose father is dead prevent her from giving a book to her husband as a gift?

A: Her brothers do not have a legal claim over her. If she is eligible to dispose of her property, her gift is valid, no matter her brothers consented or not.

*   *   *

Privileging one of her children from a different husband with a charity

Q: Is it permissible to a woman to privilege one of her children with a piece of land as a charity from her own possessions to the exclusion of the rest of her children, knowing that the stated mother died in the place that she gave to her child as a charity?

A: If the gift is not received until the death of the mother, it turns null and void. If received before that, it should be distributed among all her children.

The charity of a grandmother

Q: A woman, being of sound health and mind, gave a portion as a charity to her son out of her possessions that could be divided among the rest of the heirs. Ten years later she died. The son, in his turn, gave all that he received from his mother as a charity to his son (i.e. the grandchild of the first donor). The event of charity was legally proved in the court. Do the rest of the heirs have the right to initiate a legal action in order to invalidate such charity?

A: If the item of charity remains in the possession of the donor until he/she dies, the charity turns void according to the famous opinions of the scholars. Confirming such contract of charity in a court, however, cannot turn it valid.

If the donor delivers the charity before his death, it will be valid, provided that he gives equal portions to the rest of the heirs. Otherwise, the charity should be returned back to him. This is confirmed by the hadith narrated in the Two Sahihs by Al-Nu'man bin Bashir, who said: "My father decided to give me a slave boy as a gift. My mother, 'Umrah bint Rawahah said: I will not approve such gift unless after the Prophet (peace be upon him) witnesses it. The father then went to the Messenger of Allah (peace be upon him) and told him the story.
The Prophet (peace be upon him) said: Do you have other children? The father replied: Yes. The Prophet (peace be upon him) asked: Have you given similar gifts to them?

The father replied: No. The Prophet (peace be upon him) said: Then go and seek another witness." In another narration, the Prophet (peace be upon him) said: "Do not expect that I will witness this. I do not witness unfairness. Fear Allah and be just towards your children!"

*   *   *

The distribution of the estate

Q: A man assigned three quarters of his accommodation to his full-son as a charity, and the remaining quarter to his full-sister, Then, as the son died, the father assigned the whole accommodation to his daughter as a charity. What is the judgment of the first and the second charity?

A: If the charity of one-quarter is delivered to his full-sister, this charity then becomes the possession of her heirs after her death, not the daughter's. Thus, the donor is not entitled to transfer the property to his daughter.

*   *   *

A father seizing the possession of his married daughter after her death

Q: A married woman, who was of the age of majority, died leaving behind a father, mother and a husband. Her father then seized all her possessions that were found in her husband's house and did not give anything of it to other legal heirs. What is the judgment of this case?

A: The act of the father is not lawful. All the possessions of the deceased daughter are the right of all the legal heirs, despite the fact the such possessions were first purchased by the father. Thus, he cannot retain such possessions after her daughter's death.

*　　*　　*

Returning in a gift

Q: What is the judgment of giving a gift, then returning in it?

A: It was narrated after the Prophet (peace be upon him) that he said: "A donor cannot return in his donation except in the case of a father who gives a gift to his child." This is the opinion of Al-Shafi'i, Malik, Ahmad, and others. However, if a gift is given in return for a similar gift, or in order to fulfil an interest, then the receiver of the gift will be obliged to return it back in value or in similar property, should he cannot compensate for it.

*　　*　　*

A divorcee returning in her gift

Q: A man divorced his wife, then asked her for reconciliation. Thus her reconciled her and gave her two dinars and asked her to given him one dinar as a gift. He then divorced her. Can the divorcee return in her gift?

124

A: Yes, she can. In such case the gift is not given willingly as the husband divorced her afterwards. ***

*   *   *

A man returning in his gift which he made to his wife after her death

Q: A man made a grant of 1000 dirhams to his wife and made a document to this effect, but did not pay her in cash. The wife then died and the heirs demanded him to pay the grant. Can the husband return in his gift in such case?

A: If the man mentioned above owed no sum to the deceased wife, neither equal to this sum or what this sum can be a compensation for it, such as the case when the husband   takes anything of her possessions and promises to give her this sum in return, in this case the heirs are not entitled to the gift.

*   *   *

Remitting a husband from the dower at the wife's death

Q: A married woman brought a just male witness and a group of women and testified that she absolves her husband from the dower he owes her. Is this absolution valid?

A: If the dower is confirmed until the death illness of the wife, absolution of it is not valid, except after the consent of the remaining heirs. If the absolution of the dower was made while she was quire healthy, it is then valid. The confirmation of the absolution of the dower while the wife is healthy is to be made by a witness and an oath on the part of the husband, according to the opinion of the Hanbali Juristic School. If the wife acknowledges in her illness that she absolved her husband of the dower when she was sound health, such acknowledgment will not be regarded as valid, according to Imam Abu Hanifah, Ahmad and others. Al-Shafi'i, however, regarded it as valid. The Prophet (peace be upon him) said: "Allah has assigned a portion of inheritance for each heir entitled to it. Thus, a legal heir is not entitled to a bequest." An ill person should not give an heir more than what he is entitled to.

*   *   *

A gift given to the wife and children

Q: A woman, whose husband paid her all her dues in his lifetime, and who has children from him, was given a sum of money by her husband in return for her dower in order to spend it for the benefit of herself and her children. If a person claims that the husband owed him a sum of money equal to or more than that given to her, can she make an oath to avert injustice from her?

A: If the husband gives a gift to one of her children and the child received it, and this gift resulted in no injustice to anyone, such gift will be considered valid. No one is entitled to seize it from her. If the husband appointed his wife as a guardian of his children's share of inheritance whether he is alive or dead, while the wife is eligible to such guardianship, no one has the right to seize this from her. If she is going to take an oath, she should say that she owes nothing to the deceased.

*   *   *

A father returning in his gift to his bad son

Q: A man gave a charity to his son and made this charity in the dower of his son's wife. Later on, the father became too feeble to earn living, and his son deserted him. Can this father return in his gift?

A: Based on the fact that the father made the gift in the dower of his son's wife, he can in no way return it.

*   *   *

BEQUESTS
A bequest or an acknowledgment of a debt?

Q: A man in his death illness said: "So and so sum of money should be paid to the orphans of such and such. It was not clear whether his saying was intended to be an acknowledgement of a debt he owed or a bequest?

A: If there was an indication in the context whether he intended an acknowledgement of a debt or a bequest, the deceased's phrase should be interpreted in the light of such indication. If it cannot be distinguished, it will be considered as a bequest.

*   *

Making bequests of unequal shares to one's children

Q: A man bequeathed unequal shares to his children and brought witnesses to attest such bequest in his deathbed. Can this bequest be effective or not?

A: An ill person is not permitted to assign a bequest to some of his children, to be delivered in his lifetime or after his death, nor to acknowledge a sum of money or property to one of his children. should he does an of the above, it will not be effective, unless after the consent of the remaining heirs. This is according to the consensus of Muslim scholars. Being a witness on such kind of bequests is not permissible, as it is regarded as supporting an unfair cause. Such kind of bequests or gifts is considered one of the greatest sins that bring about destruction to it their doer. This is because a bequest or a gift of such kind most likely leads to disagreement and even hatred and enmity among the heirs.

A postponed oath

Q: A woman bequeathed one-third of her property to her daughter before her death. The father of the girl then was made her guardian. The father then made a case at the court to prove such bequest. The court ascertained the death of the testatrix, her being bequeathed to her daughter, and that her father accepted to be a guardian of such bequest. The judge, however, could not issue a judgment to prove the bequest because of the inability to let the young girl make an oath to this effect due to her minority. Should her father take an oath instead of her? Or should the judge postpone the issuance of the judgment until the girl attains majority to take the oath herself?

A: The father should not take the oath instead of her daughter, nor should the judgment be postponed until the girl attains majority. Rather, the judgment should be issued immediately. There is not disagreement among scholars on this point, so long as no legal claim is made against the father that opposes his claim.

*   *   *

Annulment of a bequest

Q: A woman made a bequest in her illness to certain persons, including her husband and her brother. Long after, she gave birth to a male child, then died. Can the bequest she made be annulled in this case?

A: All that exceeds one-third of the bequest should be returned to the heirs. As for the bequest for the husband, it is not valid, as he is entitled to inheritance. As for the brother, the bequest for him is valid, as he cannot inherit in the presence of the son. Thus, the portion bequeathed to the brother and others should not exceed one-third of the whole estate, and it is to be distributed among them according to the shares specified by the deceased.

*   *   *

Can a nephew be an heir?

Q: A woman died and left behind a nephew (son of her sister). She allocated more than one-third of her estate as a charity. Can this bequest be effected, thus giving the nephew the rest of the estate?

A: A bequest should not exceed one-third out of the entire estate. More than one-third is not permitted, unless after the consent of the legal heirs. A nephew is entitled to inherit the entire estate, according to the opinion of the scholars who give the uterine relatives the right to inherit. This   is the opinion of the majority of early Muslims (*Salaf*),   Abu Hanifah, Ahmad, a group of the Shafi'i scholars, and a variant opinion in the Maliki School, in case the public treasury is deficient.

A bequest to a husband and a paternal uncle and a grandmother

Q: A woman died and left behind a father, a paternal uncle and a grandmother. He father had claimed her majority at the court before he gave her in marriage. In her death illness, she bequeathed one-half of her estate to her husband and the other one-half to her paternal uncle, giving nothing to her father and grandmother. Is this bequest valid?

A: The bequest for the paternal uncle is valid, but should not exceed one-third, except with the consent of other heirs. The bequest for the husband, however, is totally invalid, except if the heirs accepted it. If the heirs rejected the bequest of more than one-third to the paternal uncle, the husband will be entitled to half of the estate after deducting the portion bequeathed, i.e. one-third. The grandmother and the father will be entitled to one-sixth each.

*   *   *

A bequest of Hajj

Q: Five days prior to her death, a woman bequeathed some things, including Hajj, recitation of the Holy Qur'an, charity, etc. Is her bequest applicable?

A: If she bequeathed that one-third of her estate be dedicated to finance certain acts of devotion to please

Allah, her bequest should be fulfilled, even in her death illness. If the bequest exceeds one-third of the whole estate, the increase should be excluded, except if the heirs consent. If the bequest is made for anything other than the acts of devotion, it will not be executable.

*   *   *

Benefit for the deceased

Q: A man bequeathed before his death that his wife should not give money to whomever recites Qur'an on his grave or recite Qur'anic verses and then dedicate them to him, claiming that his heart was already full of Qur'an and in need of no more. The wife knew that he could have not memorized the Holy Qur'an. Can his bequest be effective? The wife's purpose is to give money to any needy person in return for reciting Qur'anic verses and dedicating them to her husband. Is she permitted to do so?

A: The bequest of the husband should be fulfilled, since the gratuity in return for recitation of the Qur'an on the grave in a religious innovation that should be avoided. It is only acceptable if made for free. This can be elaborated as follows:

1. Hiring someone to recite Qur'anic verses and dedicate them to the deceased is not acceptable, and no reward of that will reach the deceased.

2.   Hiring someone to recite Qur'anic verses only is also a religious innovation.

3.   Hiring someone as an instructor of the Holy Qur'an is permissible.

If that woman desires to benefit her deceased husband, she may give charity on his behalf, as the reward of charity reaches the deceased, according to the unanimous agreement of scholars. If she gives charity to a group of poor reciters to fulfill their needs and enable them to give up the profession of reciting Qur'an on the graves, her charity will be rewardable and such reward will reach the deceased.

*   *   *

The guardian of the orphan girl

Q: An orphan girl has a wealth, and a person is proposing to her. Can her guardian sell some of her property to buy her the requirements of marriage that suits her social status?

A: Yes, the guardian can sell some of her property to buy her all necessities of the wedding on equitable terms.

IHERITANCE
The share of the widow

Q: What is the share of the widow of the inheritance of her deceased husband, knowing that he left behind children?

A: The widow is entitled to her dower and all liabilities the husband owed her, just like other creditors. After deducting the amounts of debt and executable bequest out of the total of the estate, the wife is entitled to one-eighth of the estate due to the presence of the children.

*　　*　　*

The share of the husband from the inheritance of his deceased wife

Q: A woman died leaving behind a husband and two parents. The father seized her estate, claiming that his deceased daughter was not major. Is the husband entitled to inherit her?

A: The estate of the deceased wife is to be distributed as follows:

> One-half for the husband,
> One third for the father, and
> One-sixth for the mother. This is according to

the view of the Four Juristic Schools, no matter she was major or not.

How to distribute the estate?

Q: Give each of the following heirs his/her share of inheritance:

A husband, grandmother, full-brothers and a son?

A:

The husband is entitled to one-fourth,

The grandmother is entitled to one-sixth,

The son is entitled to the remaining portion of the estate,

The full brothers receive nothing.

*　　　*　　　*

The sisters and the daughters

Q: A woman died leaving behind a husband, two daughters, a mother, and two full-sisters. Are the sisters entitled to a share of inheritance?

A: the question is to be divided as follows:

The husband is entitled to one-fourth,

The mother is entitled to one-sixth,

The two daughters are entitled to two-thirds,

The full-sisters will receive nothing in the presence of the daughters. This is according to the consensus of the Four Juristic Schools.

Paternal and maternal brothers and sisters

Q: A woman died leaving behind a husband, mother, full-sister and a paternal brother and sister. Give each his/her share of inheritance?

A: The question consists of ten shares, originally six, but turns to ten by virtue of the application of the scheme of distribution called 'Awl. The question is called "Dhat Al-Furukh" [the Mother of the Chicks,] due to the so many resort to the scheme of 'Awl in it.

The husband is entitled to half of the estate,

The mother is entitled to one-sixth as a share,

The full-sister is entitled to three shares,

The paternal sister is entitled to one-sixth in order to complete the share of the two-thirds with the full-sister. The two maternal brother and sister are entitled to one-third as two shares. The total thus is ten shares. This is according to the consensus of the Muslim scholars.

*   *   *

A husband, mother and maternal sister

Q: A woman died leaving behind a husband, mother, and maternal sister. What is the share of each of inheritance?

A: This question is to be divided into eleven shares:

> The daughter is entitled six shares,
>
> The husband is entitled to three shares,
>
> The mother is entitled to two shares,
>
> The maternal sister receives nothing, as she

cannot inherit in the presence of the daughter. This is according to the agreement of the majority of scholars, including those who approve of the scheme of Radd distribution, such as Abu Hanifah and Ahmad. As for those who do not approve of the Radd scheme of distribution, they divide the question into twelve shares:

> Six shares for the daughter,
>
> Two shares for the husband, and the twelfth

share should be dedicated to the public treasury.

*

A daughter, maternal brother and a male cousin

Q: A woman died leaving behind a daughter, maternal brother and a male cousin. What is the share of each from the estate?

A:

> The daughter is entitled to one-half,
>
> The male cousin is entitled to the remaining

portion of the estate,

> The maternal brother receives nothing.

However, it is preferable to give him some consideration if

he witnesses the distribution of the estate. His is according to the opinions of the Imams of the Four Juristic Schools.

*   *   *

A husband, father, mother, son and daughter

Q: A woman died leaving behind a husband, father, mother, son and daughter. After her death, her father died, leaving behind a father, sister, grandfather and a grandmother. Give each heir his share, bearing in mind the necessary changes after the death of the father?

A:

The husband is entitled to one-fourth,

The two parents are entitled to two-sixths,

The remaining portion of the estate goes to the son and daughter, one-third each. Then estate of the father is to be distributed as follows:

One-sixth for the grandmother,

The remaining portion of the estate goes to the father (i.e. the grandfather of the first deceased).

The sister will get nothing, nor the grandfather, as both do not inherit in the presence of the father.

*   *   *

The distribution of the estate between the husband and the nephew

Q: A woman died leaving behind a husband and a nephew, what the share of each of them in her estate?

A: The husband is entitled to one-half of the estate. As for the nephew, according to one view, he is entitled to the remaining portion of the estate. This is the opinion of Imam Abu Hanifah and his companions, the famous opinion of Imam Ahmad, and a group of the Shafi'i companions.

The second opinion:

The remaining portion of the estate is to be dedicated to the public treasury, which is the opinion of many of the companions of Imam Al-Shafi'i.

The origin of this question is a difference which occurred among the Muslim scholars concerning the inheritance of the uterine relatives who have no prescribed Qur'anic shares of inheritance, or according to the scheme of ta'sib. The opinion of Imam Malik, Imam Al-Shafi'i and famous narration after Imam Ahmad is that the deceased who leaves behind no heirs entitled to the prescribed Qur'anic shares, or inheritance by virtue of the scheme of ta'sib, his estate should go the public treasury.

This opinion of most earlier scholars, Imam Abu Hanifah, Imam Al-Thauri, Imam Ishaq, and Imam Ahmad bin Hanbal is that the remaining portion goes to the uterine relatives, as the Holy Qur'an says what means: **"Blood-relations among each other have closer personal ties, in the Book of Allah..."** (33:6) The Prophet (peace be upon him) said: "The maternal uncle is the heir of the deceased who left behind no other relatives. He is to inherit his estate (when he dies) and to ransom him (if he falls in captivity)."

The daughters of one's brother

Q: A man died leaving behind a wife, a full-sister and three daughters of his brother. Are the daughters of his brother entitled to inherit him? If yes, what are their shares of inheritance?

A:

The wife is entitled to one-fourth,

The full-sister is entitled to one-half, the daughters of his son receive nothing, and the remaining one-fourth goes to the nearest male relative (asabah), otherwise it is to be returned to the full-sister, or be given to the public treasury.

*   *   *

A divorced-thrice-widow

Q: A man had suffered from a chronic disease for three months. He asked his wife to bring him a drink, but she did not bring him the drink immediately. He in turn said to her: "You are divorced thrice". She still lived with him to serve him and take care of him. Twenty years later, he died. Is the divorce effective? Can his oath be broken on such-like case? Are the heirs rightful to disinherit his divorced wife?

A: The divorce is effective, so long as the husband is of sound mind and made it with fee will. However, the divorced wife is entitled to inherit, according to the opinion of Imam Malik, Imam Ahmad, Imam Abu Hanifah, and the earlier opinion of Imam Al-Shafi'i. 'Uthman bin 'Affan (may Allah be pleased with him) applied this judgment in the case of the wife of 'Abdul-Rahamn bin 'Auf, whom the latter divorced in his death illness. 'Uthman gave her the right to inherit from Ibn 'Auf's estate. She should count her 'Iddah (waiting period) according to the longest of the two terms of 'Iddah: the 'Iddah for divorce or the 'Iddah for the death of her husband. If the husband becomes insane, his divorce is ineffective.

*　　*　　*

Divorce before consummation of marriage

Q: A man divorced his wife once before consummating marriage with her, while his being in death illness. Can this be regarded as a contrivance on the part of the husband to disinherit his wife, thus be treated in a manner to spoil his plot and preserve to the wife her right of inheritance and the full amount of her dower? Or she is to be deprived from the inheritance, but be entitled to half of her dower?

A: According to the opinion of the majority of scholars, the woman divorced after the consummation of marriage shall be entitled to inherit from her husband. Thus passed the judgment of Caliph 'Uthman bin 'Affan (may Allah be pleased with him) in the case of Tumadur bint Al-Asbagh, the wife of the Companion 'Abdul-Rahman bin 'Auf (may Allah be pleased with him), who divorced her in his death illness. This is also the opinion of Imam Malik, Imam Abu Hanifah and Imam Al-Shafi'i in his earlier opinion.

As for the woman whose 'Iddah ends, and the one who is divorced before the consummation of marriage, there are two opinions for the scholars in this, the more correct of which is that the wife will be entitled to inheritance in these cases also. This is the opinion of Imam Malik, the famous narration after Imam Ahmad and the opinion of Imam Al-Shafi'i. It was reported that the Caliph 'Uthman bin 'Affan (may Allah be pleased with him) judged that a woman in such case will be entitled to inheritance, even after the completion of her 'Iddah. This judgment is based on the fact that a husband in his death illness is considered as legally interdicted, in the sense that his disposition will not be effective, should it badly affect the rights of the wife or any of the heirs.

*　　*　　*

A husband who divorces his wife before his death in a way to disinherit her

Q: A man divorced his wife in his death illness, three days before his death to disinherit her. Is this divorce effective? What is the share she is entitled to in his estate?

A: If divorce is revocable and the husband dies while the wife is in her 'Iddah (waiting period), she is entitled to inheritance, according to the consensus of the Muslim scholars. If the divorce is irrevocable, the wife is also entitled to inheritance.

Thus judged the Caliph 'Uthman bin 'Affan (may Allah be pleased with him) in the case of Tumadur bint Al-Asbagh, the wife of the Companion 'Abdul-Rahman bin 'Auf, who divorced her thrice in his death illness. 'Uthman (may Allah be pleased with him) consulted the Companions in her case and they told him that the wife in such case was entitled to inherit from her husband.

The disagreement on this question appeared during the rule of Ibn Al-Zubair (may Allah be pleased with him), who said: "In his place (meaning 'Uthman) I would have not given her (the wife of 'Abdul-Rahamn bin 'Auf) a right to inherit." However, consensus of the opinions of scholars had already been concluded before Ibn Al-Zubair became a *mujtahid*.

This was the opinion of the leading Successors and latter scholars. It is also the opinion of the people of Iraq, such as Imam Al-Thauri, Imam Abu Hanifah and his companions, the people of Median, such as Imam Malik and his companions, the jurists of Hadith, such as Imam Ahmad bin Hanbal and others. This also was the earlier opinion of Imam Al-Shafi'i. In his later opinion, he agreed with Ibn Al-Zubair. To them both, the divorce in the above question is effective, as if it was the wife who died, the husband would have not inherited her. Just like this, the wife is not entitled to inherit him. Through divorce the woman became unlawful to her husband: he cannot have intercourse with her or seek pleasure with her. Thus, she becomes like a stranger woman to him, thus does not inherit.

The majority of Muslim scholars provided that the property of a man who is in his death illness is attached to the disposition of his heirs. He will not be entitled to dispose of it in a way to disinherit some of the heirs or prefer some of them to the others. He is not entitled to make a donation to a non-relative with more than one-third in his death illness.

In a hadith it was narrated: "Whoever cuts an inheritance, Allah will cut his inheritance in Paradise." (a weak hadith). Concerning the 'Iddah, there is a disagreement of opinions, but the soundest is that a woman divorced by her husband in his death illness should observe the waiting period according to the longest of the two terms (i.e. the term of 'Iddah for a divorced woman or the 'Iddah for a widow). Concerning her dower, there are two opinions, the preferred of which is that she is entitled to dower also.

MARRIAGE

Proposing to marry a woman already engaged to another person

Q: Is it permissible to a man to propose to a woman already engaged to another person?

A: It was narrated in the Two Sahihs after the Prophet (peace be upon him) that he said: "It is not lawful for a man to propose to a woman already engaged to his brother (Muslim) or to indulge in a bargain already concluded by his brother (Muslim). Thus the Four Juristic Schools agreed that it is unlawful to propose to a woman already engaged to another person.

A disagreement, however, arose concerning the validity of the marriage of the second suitor:
1.	According to Imam Malik and Imam Ahmad in one of the two narrations after him, such marriage is not valid.
2.	According to Imam Abu Hanifah, Imam Al-Shafi'i and the second narration after Imam Ahmad, such marriage is valid. This opinion is based on the fact that what is unlawful is the proposal, not the contract of marriage. The first opinion is based on the argument that as the contract of marriage is the result of the proposal, which in invalid, the contract of marriage itself turns invalid by way of analogy. There is no disagreement,

however, on the point that one who propose to a woman already engaged to another is a sinner.

* * *

A woman proposed to during her 'Iddah (waiting period)

Q: A suitor proposed to a divorced woman in her 'Iddah and supported her financially. What is the judgment on this?

A: It is not lawful to explicitly propose to a woman in her 'Iddah of divorce. It is not even lawful to propose to a widow in her 'Iddah, following the death of her husband. Both the suitor and the fiancée should be given a deterrent punishment and should be hindered to marry one another, a punishment which is contrary to their purpose.

* * *

Muhallil (a man who married a woman then divorces her so that she may return to her previous husband who irrevocably divorced her)

Q: A man divorced his wife thrice. After the completion of her 'Iddah, she married and then was divorced on the same day. Her ex-husband did not know about her second marriage and then her divorce except after two days. Is he permitted to return her after the completion of the 'Iddah of divorce?

A: The ex-husband is not permitted to propose to his ex-wife during her 'Iddah, following her divorce from her second husband. If divorce is revocable, he cannot propose to her implicitly either. But if the divorce is irrevocable, the implicit proposal is disagreed upon among the Muslim scholars. These judgments apply if the second marriage was not prearranged by either the ex-husband or his ex-wife in order to return to return to each other. This kind of marriage is known as "Muhallil marriage". The Prophet (peace be upon him) said: "May Allah curse the Muhallil and the one for whom Muhallil is procured."

*   *   *

The second proposal

Q: A suitable suitor proposed to a woman and agreed with her father on the amount of dower, which was in two portions, one was to be paid before marriage and one deferred. The first portion was paid to the father throughout a period of four years. Meanwhile, the suitor supported the family of his fiancée financially. No written document is there to prove the amounts paid b the suitor. Another suitor then proposed to the same woman and offered a greater amount of dower and hindered the first suitor from marriage. What is the judgment on this?

A: It is not lawful for a man to propose to a woman already engaged to another and such engagement is accepted by the guardian of the fiancée. In a hadith the Prophet (peace be upon him) said: "It is not lawful for a man to propose to a woman already engaged to his brother (Muslim)." Whoever does this, or supports others in doing this, should be punished a deterring punishment.

Private meeting of a man with a woman

Q: Is it permissible to a man to meet in private with the wife of his husband and his female cousins?

A: It is not permissible to a man to meet in private with the wife of his brother or with his female cousins. However, if he is accompanied by others in this meeting, and no suspicion is feared, it is the permissible.

* * *

The divorced thrice

Q: A man divorced his wife thrice. They have two children. The wife has been residing in the house of the husband for two years following the divorce. Is she permitted to eat from his food? Is she still considered under his control?

A: A woman divorced thrice becomes forbidden to her ex-husband, just as any other woman. He is not entitled to have private meetings with her or to look at parts of her body, which he is not permitted to see from other women, whom he can marry. He, further, has no control over her. He is not permitted to agree with her to marry another man then be divorced from that man and in order to return to him. He is not permitted also to give her an outlay in return for this. If she marries another man in a way known to all Muslims, then her new husband dies, or divorces her thrice, the ex-husband cannot propose to her in her 'Iddah.

This is according to the consensus of Muslim scholars. Allah the Almighty said what means: **"There is no blame on you if ye make an indirect offer of betrothal or hold it in your hearts. Allah knows that ye cherish them in your hearts; but do not make a secret contracts with them that you speak to them in terms honorable,..."** (2:253)

In this case the ex-husband is strongly forbidden to conclude a marriage contract with the woman until the term of 'Iddah is completed.

The proxy of a dhimmi in marriage of a Muslim

Q: A man appointed a dhimmi person to be his representative in accepting marriage with a Muslim woman. Is this kind of marriage valid?

A: Disagreement has arisen concerning this question. A representative in proxy marriage should be one whose acceptance of marriage for himself is valid. If one appoints a woman, a minor child, or an insane person to be his representative in a proxy marriage, such marriage will not be valid. If a representative is such one whose deputy acceptance of marriage is not permitted unless after the approval of his guardian, such as the case of a slave, there are two opinions concerning this, ascribed to Imam Ahmad and others. If his acceptance of marriage is valid without taking a permission from another person, such as the case when a female-salve is sought in marriage by a representative who cannot legally marry her, such kind of proxy will be valid.

As for choosing a dhimmi person to be one's representative in the proxy marriage, this case resembles the case when a dhimmi person gives in marriage his dhimmi daughter to a Muslim. If he marries her to a dhimmi person, such marriage will be valid. But if he marries her to a Muslim, there are two opinions concerning this case in the Juristic School of Imam Ahmad bin Hanbal and others.

The first opinion is that such kind of marriage will be valid. The second opinion is to the contrary. Based on the second opinion, a Muslim who marries a dhimmi woman by proxy should appoint a Muslim representative. It was also said that such match cannot be concluded except by the ruler, as he is considered a guardian for all Muslim men and women in the question of marriage.

As for the opinion that provides that all the above solutions are permissible, it is founded on the argument that the ownership by virtue of the contract of marriage is realized to the husband not to the representative, but this is not the case in other types of contracts.

The Muslim jurists differed over this last question: Imam Al-Shafi'i, Imam Ahmad and others are of the opinion that the rights of the contact of marriage are related to the representative, but the ownership resulted from the contract is related to the husband, who is the Muslim seeker of representation.

The dhimmi representative in lieu of a Muslim in a marriage contract resembles a representative who cannot marry the woman whom he is made a representative to conclude the contract of marriage with her, such as her maternal uncle, who can be a representative in her marriage, but cannot himself marry her. But it is preferable not to make a dhimmi person a representative to a Muslim in marriage contracts.

It is desirable to conclude the contract of marriage in a mosque, as it was narrated that: "Whoever witnesses the marriage of a Muslim, is like one who witnessed a conquest in the cause of Allah." Thus, according to the opinion of Ahmad and others, the contract should be concluded in Arabic.

A disbeliever should not be a representative to a Muslim in a proxy marriage contract, but if it happens the contract will be valid, since there not legal proof to claim its being invalid.

*   *   *

Marriage in illness

Q: A man married while his being ill. Is his contract of marriage valid?

A: The marriage concluded by an ill person is valid, and his wife will be entitled to inherit him and to receive the portion of dower equal to her counterparts in her family, without any increase. This is according to the consensus of the Muslim jurists.

*   *   *

A woman marrying with a guardian other than her father

Q: A man has a daughter who has not attained maturity yet. She was married without a guardian in the absence of her father, claiming that the father was dead and presenting her maternal uncle as her brother. Is this contract of marriage valid or not?

A: If the maternal was attested to be her brother, such attestation will be regarded as false. This way the maternal uncle cannot be regarded as a guardian to her. Rather, the marriage will be considered to concluded without the presence of the guardian of the bride, which means that it is null, according to most of the Muslim scholars and jurists, such as Imam Al-Shafi'i, Imam Ahmad and others. The father may renew this contract of marriage if he likes. The one who witnessed that her maternal uncle is her brother and that her father is dead will be considered as making a false testimony and should be punished a discretionary punishment as well as the maternal uncle. If this marriage is consummated, the wife will be entitled to the entire amount of dower, should it is put to an end. The father has the right to marry her during the 'Iddah (waiting period) of such invalid marriage. The is according to the opinion of Imam Abu Hanifah, Imam Al-Shafi'i and the famous opinion of Imam Ahmad bin Hanbal.

A lying woman who changes her name and the name of her father

Q: A woman has a father and a brother. In the absence of her father, though the representative of her father who was deputized in marriage and other affairs was present, she brought witnesses and changed her name and the name of her father and claimed that she had been divorced by an ex-husband who then wanted to marry her again. She, further, brought a stranger and claimed that he was her brother. After the witnesses make their testimony, the whole matter was disclosed.

Is such woman liable to a discretionary punishment that should be executed by the ruler or one of the local authorities, such as the muhtasib?

A: This woman is liable to a discretionary punishment, even for several times, which is preferable. The Caliph 'Umar bin Al-Khattab used to repeat the discretionary punishment for committing something forbidden.

Thus he was of the habit of giving the guilty person 100 slashes on the first day, 100 on the second and 100 on the third, so as to avoid the damage of any of the body members of the guilty person, should he receives all the 300 lashes all at one time.

The woman in the above case committed some major sins such as ascribing oneself to a man other than one's real father, and made a stranger man take the place of her brother. In the Two Sahihs it was narrated after the Prophet (peace be upon him): "Whoever attributes himself to a man other than his father, or be loyal to people other than his maters (if he is a slave), Allah will curse him, as well as the angel and all mankind."

In another hadith the Prophet (peace be upon him) said: "Whoever ascribes himself to a man other that his father, the Paradise will be forbidden to him." In a third hadith it was narrated that the Prophet (peace be upon him) said: "He will not belong to us who knowingly claims his being a son to a man other than his real father, for such person will be a disbeliever. He will not belong to us who claims something which is not really his own, but let him be seated in his place in the hell-fire. Whoever wrongfully accuses another of disbelief, will be a transgressor against him." These two strong words indicate that the one guilty of any of these will be liable to a strong punishment of no less than 100 lashes.

Even worse, the above-mentioned woman deceived the witnesses and led them to witness an invalid contract, and married with a null contract. According to Muslim scholars, a marriage contract will be regarded void if concluded in the absence of the guardian. They used to inflict a discretionary punishment on whomever is guilty of this crime, in pursuit of the example of the Caliph 'Umar bin Al-Khattab (may Allah be pleased with him). This is the opinion of Imam Al-Shafi'i and others.

Rather, some group of scholars were of the opinion the punishment of stoning to death should be executed in suchlike cases. Even those who claimed that marriage without a guardian is permissible did not approve of the ascription to a false father or of bringing a false guardian. Thus the punishment of such acts was agreed upon among all Muslim scholars.

That woman is liable to punishment also because of her telling lies, and the claim that the man she brought was her ex-husband who had divorced her. The fake husband also is to be punished, as well as the one who pretended that he was her brother. As for the witnesses who knew their case, they will be liable to the punishment of perjury which included the witness of her false attribution to other than the woman's father, the fabricated stories of divorce and marriage, and the absence of the real guardian.

The punishment of those people should be intensified. The Muslims scholars maintained that the face of a perjurer should be blackened as an indication that he blackened his face by telling lies, and should be made to ride a mount on a reversed position (his face to the posterior of the mount and his back to its face), as an indication that he reversed the correct narration. He is to be roamed with throughout the streets of the city to be defamed among people.

The discretionary punishment can be carried out by the ruler, the muhtasib or any other influential capable of inflicting it.

In this case the infliction of punishment is necessary, since it includes the corruption of women and the false testimony. The Prophet (peace be upon him said: "If people witnessed evil behavior widespread and did not try to change it, it will be very likely that Allah will cover all with a torture."

Obligation of the virgin major woman

Q: Can a father compel hi s virgin major daughter to marry a certain person?

A: There are two opinions concerning this:

1.   The father has the right to compel his virgin daughter to marry a certain person. This is the opinion of Imam Malik and Imam Al-Shafi`i, and the chosen opinion of Al-Kharaqi and Al-Qadi and his companions.

2.   The father does not have the right to compel his virgin daughter to marry a certain person, which is the opinion of Abu Hanifah and others, and the chosen opinion of Abu Bakr 'Abdul-'Aziz bin Ja'far. This is the correct opinion. Difference arose, however, on the cause of obligation on the part of the father: the daughter being virgin only, minor only, or for both reasons. The correct view is that the father will be entitled to compel his daughter if she is a minor. Thus, a virgin major woman cannot be obliged to marry.

It was narrated after the Prophet (peace be upon him) that he said: "A virgin woman cannot be married unless she gives her consent. As for a previously married woman, she should agree on marriage." It was said to him: A virgin woman becomes shay to give consent. He (peace be upon him) said: Her silence is regarded as a consent." In another wording of the narration it was said: "She (the virgin woman) cannot be given in marriage until her permission is sought." This means that the father, or anyone in his place should seek her permission.

3.   The father, furthermore, cannot dispose of the property of his major daughter unless after taking her permission. However, her chastity, is of greater value than her property.

4.   Furthermore, according to the consensus of opinion of Muslim scholars, it is the minority, not virginity that gives the father the right to interdict the disposition of her daughter.

5.   Those who give the father the right of obligation differed on the case when a woman chooses a man, who is equal ho her status as a husband, while the father chooses another person, who is equal to her status also, as a husband. Which of the two choices is to prevail? Those who say that the choice of the father is to prevail, which is one of the two views in the Shafi'i school, they actually contradict the original rule in their school. As for those who gave preference to the choice of the father, their opinion includes a crystal-clear corruption and harm. The Prophet (peace be upon him) said: "A previously married woman (*thaiyyb*) is more rightful to dispose of her own affairs than her guardian, and the virgin woman is to give her consent (before her guardian proceeds on the affair of her marriage).

Her silence is an indication of her consent." In another narration it was said: "The previously married woman (*thaiyyb*) is more rightful to manage her own affairs than her guardian." This indicates, on the other hand, that a virgin is not entitled to dispose of her own affairs without the interference of her guardian. Rather, the guardian is more rightful to that than her. This is the exclusive right of her father and grandfather. This is the argument of the proponents of giving the right of obligation in marriage to 6the guardian. They did not apply the surface meaning of the above hadith and stuck to their own understanding of it, though they could not understand the purport of the Prophet's saying: "The previously married woman (*aiyym*) is more rightful to dispose of her own affairs than her guardian, which is applicable for any kind of guardian, not only the father and the grandfather as they claim.

As for the Prophet's saying: "The virgin woman is to give her consent (as regards her marriage)", they held that ascertaining the consent of the virgin is not obligatory, rather mandatory. Some of them said that: "As the consent of the virgin is mandatory, it is sufficient to interpret her silence as a consent. If it is obligatory, she should have been obliged to express her consent in speech." This is what some of the companions of Imam Al-Shafi'i and Imam Ahmad said.

The above opinion, however, is contradictory with the preceding consensus of Muslim scholars, and the clear sayings of the Prophet (peace be upon him). It is proved by the sound detailed texts from the Prophetic Sunnah and th consensus of opinion of Muslim scholars that if a virgin woman is married by her brother or her paternal uncle, her consent should be ascertained.

Actually, the Prophet (peace be upon him) differentiated between the virgin and the previously married woman, as mentioned in the above hadith, in terms of the methods of ascertaining the consent of each in the case of marriage, i.e. silence for the first and speech for the second. The Prophet (peace be upon him) did not differentiate between them in terms of the principle of compulsion (*Ijbar*).

Forcing a virgin woman to marry against her will is contradictory to the teachings of Islam and the dictates of sound logic. The guardian of a virgin is not entitled to force her to conclude a sale or tenancy contract against her will, or to compel her to eat, drink or wear a dress which she does not want. How can then he oblige her to live and have intercourse with a man that she is averse to. The friendliness, intimacy and mercy, which are the prime aims of marriage, cannot be realized in suchlike kind of marriage.

If a discord (*Shiqaq*) occurs between the spouse, two arbiters (*hakamain*) should be appointed, one from the family of the husband and the other from the family of the wife. According to some opinion, those two persons are regarded as representatives of the spouse, but not arbiters. But the correct view is the first. The mission of the arbiters is to exert their efforts to realize the interest of the spouse, either to reconcile or separate each from the other. Thus, one of the arbiters is entitled to the right of divorce without the permission of the husband, while the second arbiter is entitled to pay a compensation from the money of the wife without taking her permission, so that the husband may divorce her. In this case the two arbiters are regarded as guardians of the spouse. Based on this opinion, a father can divorce the wife of his minor or insane son, if he deems an interest in doing so.

Likewise, a father can conclude Khul' on behalf of his daughter if he deems an interest din doing so.

Moreover, if a woman is divorced before the consummation of marriage, her father can remit the husband from half of the amount of the dower, if he is considered as the one entitled to conclude the contract of marriage, which is the opinion of Imam Malik, and one of the two narrations, after Imam Ahmad. The Qur'an supports this opinion.

The dower differs in nature from the rest of the woman's property, as it is due to her as a gift. In the case of divorce before the consummation of marriage, the woman does not lose her virginity, and divorce in considered as an annulment of the marriage, just like other kinds of contracts, thus half the dower was not originally the right of the divorcee. But the Law-Giver made it her right as a compensation of the mental anguish resulted from the divorce.

According to Ibn 'Umar, Imam Al-Shafi'i and Imam Ahmad, in one of the narrations after him, half of the amount of the dower in the case of divorce before the consummation of marriage is the equivalent of the *Mut'ah* (outlay and all that is given by the man to his divorced woman to benefit with) in the case of divorce after the consummation of marriage.

According to Imam Ahmad (in another narration after him) and Imam Abu Hanifah, the *Mut'ah* is the exclusive right of the woman who is divorced before the determination of the amount of dower and the consummation of marriage. According to them, *Mut'ah* is a compensation given to the divorcee instead of half of the amount of dower.

Others say that the dower becomes a settled right to the woman by virtue of the conclusion of the contract of marriage and the consummation of it, even before divorce. As the *Mut'ah* is the result of divorce, it will be a right to every divorcee, except in the case of the woman who is divorced after the determination of the amount of dower, but before the consummation of marriage. In such case she is given half of the amount of dower as a *Mut'ah*, thus will not be entitled to any increase. This opinion is stronger, as the Mut'ah is made as the result of divorce, so it should not be made a compensation of the dower, which is the result of the conclusion of the contract of marriage and the consummation of it.

A third opinion, which is attributed to another narration after Imam Ahmad provides that each divorcee is entitled to Mut'ah, as is maintained in the following Qur'anic verse: **"O you who believe! When you marry believing women, and then divorce them before you have sexual intercourse with them, no 'Iddah [divorce prescribed period] have you to count in respect of them. So give them a present, and set the free (i.e. divorce), in a handsome manner."** (33:49)

The command in the verse provides for the Mut'ah for women divorced before the consummation of marriage. The case of divorce determining the amount of dower was not specified here, despite the fact that in most cases divorce occurs after determining the amount of dower.

In addition to the above-mentioned, if divorce is the cause of *Mut'ah*, the dower is the result of the contract of marriage. As for the woman who gives her husband the right to determine the amount of her dower, without actually determining it, she will be entitled to the same amount of dower paid to any of her counterparts in her family upon the conclusion of the contract of marriage. It will be her settled right even after the death of her husband. In a hadith it was narrated that a woman married to a man, then her husband died before determining her dower.

The Prophet (peace be upon him) decided that she would be entitled to an amount of dower similar to that paid to any of her peers in her family, without decrease or increase. However, if such woman was divorced before the consummation of marriage, she would not have been entitled to half of the dower, in accordance to the Qur'anic verse, since she did not stipulate the determination of the amount of dower. The anguish resulted to her by divorce is compensated by *Mut'ah*.

The purpose of the Law-Giver is not to compel a woman to marry a man against her will. Rather, in the case of discord, the woman's affair is managed by persons other than the husband, from among her family and his, in order to fulfil the interest of both of them. Such persons can separate the wife from her husband without his permission. How can she then be obliged to live with him against her will?

The wife is considered as optionally captivated in the house of her husband. Thus, such captivity cannot be concluded without her consent. The Prophet (peace be upon him) said: "Fear Allah as regards women. They are regarded as captives in your houses. You have taken them by virtue of the trust of Allah. They have become lawful to you (to intercourse with) by virtue of the Word of Allah."

*   *   *

Marrying a woman to her relative against her will

Q: A major woman had a relative who proposed to marry her, but she refused him. Her family said to the relative: "Conclude the marriage while her father is present." Can this marriage be effective?

A: No doubt, if the relative is not suitable to marry her, she will not be compelled to marry him. If he is suitable, the scholars have two opinions as regards this case, the stronger of which, which finds support in the Holy Qur'an and the Prophetic Sunnah is that she will not be obliged to accept this marriage. The Prophet (peace be upon him) said: "A virgin woman cannot be married unless after her father ascertains her consent, which can be indicated by her silence."

*   *   *

Guardianship of a stranger

Q: A man married a major woman from her paternal grandfather, who neither claimed his granddaughter as major nor had a permission from her father to be her guardian. Short before his death, the grandfather appointed a stranger as a guardian of his granddaughter. Is the grandfather still considered a guardian of the woman after her marriage? Is he entitled to appoint a guardian to her?

A: If the woman is major and mature, no one can consider himself her guardian, neither the grandfather, nor any other person. This is according to the consensus of the Muslim scholars.

If she is liable to be interdicted, the scholars differed on her case as follows:

Imam Abu Hanifah deems that the grandfather has the right to be her guardian.

According to Imam Malik and the famous opinion of Imam Ahmad, the grandfather is not entitled to be her guardian.

*   *   *

WOMEN FORBIDDEN IN MARRIAGE
The Exchange Marriage [*Shighar*]

Q: A group of people used to exchange female relatives in marriage, that a man gives his sister in marriage to a person on the condition that such person should in turn gives him his sister or daughter in marriage. If either of the two men spends money on his household, the other spends equal amount of money. If one brings clothes to his wife, the other follows suit. The matter goes the same in all things. If one is angry with his wife, the other becomes angry too. If one is pleased with his wife, the other becomes happy too. If the former punishes his wife, the latter punishes his wife too. Is such conduct permissible?

A: Each of the two husbands should live with his wife on equitable terms, or better divorce her with an agreeable manner. A husband should not vary his treatment to his wife on the basis of the treatment of the other husband. A wife is entitled to a right on her husband, which does not fall due to a maltreatment on the part of her brother or her father. If one of the two husbands deals with his wife with injustice, the other should prove his accountability on this, rather than being unfair to his wife, for the mere reason that she is the daughter of the other one. If both husbands deal with their wives with injustice, aiming to revenge each other, they both will be liable to punishment. The wife of each will be entitled to demand her rights from her husband. If such treatment is stipulated in the contract of marriage, it will be considered an invalid condition attributed to the exchange marriage [*Shighar*].

*   *   *

Combining a woman and her maternal aunt in marriage

Q: A man married the maternal aunt of another, then married his daughter. Is this marriage valid?

A: It is not permissible to combine in marriage the maternal aunt of a man along with his daughter. The Prophet (peace be upon him) forbade that a woman be taken in marriage along with her maternal or paternal aunt. This is agreed upon by the Four Imams. They also agreed that the above hadith includes the maternal aunt of the father, mother and grandmother, as well as the paternal aunts of the parents. Thus, a man cannot take in marriage a woman along with the maternal aunt of her father or mother.

*   *   *

Taking in marriage the paternal aunt of a man along with his niece

Q: A man took in marriage the maternal aunt of a man along with the niece of that man. Is this marriage valid?

A: Taking both of these women in marriage at the same time is considered as combining a woman and the maternal aunt of her father in marriage. If the father of the woman is a maternal or a full-brother of the other man, then the maternal uncle of one of them is the maternal uncle of the other. But if the former is the paternal brother of the latter, then the maternal aunt of one of them cannot be regarded the maternal aunt of the other, rather, she is regarded his paternal aunt. In all case, combining a woman and the maternal aunt of her mother, the paternal aunt of her father, or mother is like combining in marriage a woman and her paternal or maternal aunt. All these forms of marriage are forbidden according to the consensus of Muslim scholars.

If a man marries either of these women after the other, the second marriage will be invalid, even without divorce. The contract of such marriage does not give the wife the right to the amount of dower or inheritance of the husband. The husband cannot consummate marriage or have intercourse with her. If marriage is already consummated, he should separate with her, just as he separates with a stranger woman.

If he wants to marry the second woman, he should divorce the first and wait until her 'Iddah (waiting period) ends. If he marries the second during the 'Iddah of the first, who is revocably divorced, such marriage will be invalid. This is the opinion of the Four Imams. If divorce is irrevocable, the marriage will be invalid also, according to the opinion of Imam Abu Hanifah and Imam Ahmad, but will be considered valid according to the opinion of Imam Malik and Imam Al-Shafi'i. If the first woman is divorced once or twice without compensation, such divorce will be considered revocable, thus marrying the second woman cannot be concluded until the completion of the 'Iddah of the first woman, according to the agreement of the Four Imams.

As for the question whether he can marry the second woman, with whom he had intercourse by virtue of an unsound marriage in her 'Iddah, there are two opinions concerning this:

Imam Abu Hanifah and Imam Al-Shafi'i are of the opinion that such marriage will be valid. The second opinion, which is attributed to Imam Malik and Ahmad in one of his two narrations is that such marriage is invalid.

*   *   *

Marrying the mother of one's wife with whom marriage is not consummated

Q: A man married a woman a year ago, then divorced her before the consummation of marriage. Can he then marry the mother of his divorcee?

A: No, it is not permissible to marry the mother of his divorcee, even if he did not consummate marriage with her.

*   *   *

12 moths without menstruation!

Q: A man divorced his wife who suckles her baby. Eight months lasted after her divorce, then she married another man who lived with her for a month, then divorced her. She remained for three monthafter divorce. Throughout that period (i.e. 12 months) she did not have her menses. She then married the first husband again, who is the father of her baby. Are these two marriages valid, or just one of them?

A: Neither the first nor the second marriage is valid. She should rather complete the waiting period of the first divorce, then wait until the completion of the 'Iddah following the second divorce, then marry whomever she wants of either of the them.

*   *   *

Menstruation twice only

Q: Three years ago a man married a woman who gave birth to a son of 2 years old now. She later claimed that she married that husband following an 'Iddah that lasted for two menstruations only and the husband confirmed her

170

claim. The husband then divorced her. What is the judgment of that divorce?

A: If the husband confirmed her claim that he married her following two menstruations of her 'Iddah (which should be three) such marriage will be invalid. The husband has to separate with her. She should then complete the 'Iddah for the first divorce, then observe the 'Iddah because of intercourse she had with the second husband. If she had the third menstruation before the second husband had intercourse with her, thus 'Iddah of the first divorce will be completed.

If the second husband divorces her, she should observe 'Iddah for three menstruations. After this she can marry anew with whomever she wants. The son she had from the second husband will be regarded as legitimate and will be attributed to him, even though he was born as a result of an unsound contract of marriage, whose unsoundness was first unknown.

*

A virgin woman who is divorced thrice

Q: A man married a virgin woman then divorced her thrice without consummating marriage. Can he marry her again with a new contract of marriage?

A: A woman who is divorced thrice, with whom marriage is not consummated shall be treated the same as that with whom marriage is consummated. This is the opinion of the majority of scholars.

* * *

The marriage of a woman whose guardian is a *fasiq* [oft-sinner]

Q: A man married a woman whose guardian was a *fasiq*, who was given to earn ill-gotten money and drink alcohol. The witnesses who attended the marriage contract were like him. Can the husband return his wife after divorcing her thrice, on the grounds that the contract was not sound (due to the fact that both the guardian and witnesses are *fasiqs*?

A: if the husband divorces her thrice, his divorce will be countable. Trying to return the wife on the grounds that the contract of marriage was not sound is a kind of manipulating to transgress the limits set by Allah twice: once before the divorce and once after it. The judgment of the divorce of the unsound marriage is disagreed upon by Imam Malik and other scholars. The marriage contract concluded by a *fasiq* guardian is valid, according to the opinion of the majority of scholars.

* * *

CONDITIONS OF MARRIAGE
Fulfilling the conditions of marriage

Q: A man married a woman on the conditions that he must not marry another woman with her, or move her to another house and to keep the daughter of his wife live with her. Is he obliged to meet such conditions after the consummation of marriage? If he does not fulfill these conditions, does the wife have the right to annul marriage?

A: According to Imam Ahmad and a group of Companions and Successors, such as 'Umar bin Al-Khattab, 'Amr bin Al-'As, Shuraih the Judge, and Al-Auza'i, such kinds of conditions should be fulfilled. According to Imam Malik, if it is conditioned that if the husband marries another woman or takes a concubine, the wife will have the option either to stay with him or to separate with him, such condition will be valid. In the Two Sahihs it is narrated that the Prophet (peace be upon him) said: "The conditions that you should be very keen to fulfill are those made in marriage contracts (with which women are made lawful to you.)"

As for the condition that the daughter of the wife should live with her in the house of the husband, and his being required to afford for her, this is considered a condition of stipulating an increase of the amount of dower, which may not be well-defined. Anything undefined stipulated in marriage contract that may reach an amount equal to the dower paid to the peers of the wife or less, is permissible. However, the matter can be decided by referring to the custom and surrounding circumstances.

Should the husband not fulfil the conditions he accepted, thus marries another woman or takes a concubine, the wife will be able to annul marriage contract.

Again a question was raised concerning the execution of the annulment of marriage: is it necessary to refer to the executive authority to carry it out or not? The preferred opinion is that is not necessary to do that. However, if reference is made to an executive authority, such authority will be entitled either to acknowledge the annulment of marriage or to cancel it.

PHYSICAL DEFECTS VERSUS MARRIAGE
Can leprosy cause the annulment of marriage?

Q: A woman married to a man, and after the consummation of marriage found out that he is a leper. Is this a valid reason to annul marriage?

A: If either of the spouse is found to be physically defective, such as in the case of insanity or leprosy, the other will have the option to annul marriage. However, if the party who found out the defect in the other accepts it, no annulment is applicable in this case. If the wife annuls the marriage, knowing the defect and accepting it, she will not be entitled to take any of her trousseau. If annulment is made before the consummation of marriage, she will not be entitled to her dower. However, if it is made after the consummation of marriage, she will be entitled to the dower.

*   *   *

The *Mustahadah* [a woman suffering from continuous vaginal bleeding]

Q: A man married a virgin woman and found out that she was suffering from continuous vaginal bleeding. The family of the wife did not tell him of that defect. Can he annul the marriage and demand the amount of dower he paid from the family of the wife? Should the father and mother of the wife be made to take oaths in case they deny. Can the husband have intercourse with this wife or not?

A: According to the preferred opinion, this defect may cause the annulment of marriage for two reasons:

1. This defect makes intercourse most likely harmful.

2. Intercourse with a woman suffering from a continual vaginal bleeding is not permissible except for a necessity, according to the famous opinion of Imam Ahmad. All that prevent intercourse physically like the blockage of vagina, or mentally like insanity incurs the annulment of marriage according to Imam Malik and Imam Al-Shafi'i. It was also reported after 'Umar bin AL-Khattab. As for complete prevention from intercourse. such as the case of the presence of impurity in the vagina. it is considerably disagreed upon among scholars. The case

of the woman who suffers from continuous vaginal bleeding, is severer than other similar cases.

If the husband annuls marriage before the consummation of marriage, he will not be required to pay the dower. If he annuls marriage after consummation, it is said that dower is payable by virtue of such case of privacy with the wife. If he had intercourse with her, he should demand the amount of dower from the party who deceived him. It is said also that the dower will not be payable by virtue of the privacy. Rather, the husband has the right to let the party who deceived him make an oath to the contrary of his claim.

Intercourse with a *Mustahadah* is considerably disagreed upon by scholars. In an opinion attributed to Al-Shafi'i and others, it was said that it is permissible to have intercourse with the *Mustahadah*. According to another opinion, having intercourse with a *Mustahadah* is not permissible except for a necessity. If the husband has intercourse with her after that, it will be counted as an acceptance on his part and will not be opted to annul marriage, if he claims his being ignorant of that, this case is disagreed upon among scholars: whether he has the option to annul marriage or not. Th preferred opinion, however, is that he has the option to do so.

A woman found to be virgin

Q: A man married a woman, knowing that she was virgin, then found out later that she was not. Can he annul marriage? Can he demand the dower he paid from the party who deceived him?

A: The husband in this case is entitled to annul marriage. Should he wants to consummate marriage, he will be entitled to demand a reduction of the mount of dower to equal the customary dower paid to a previously married woman. If he annuls marriage before consummation, he will not be required to pay a dower.

*   *   *

ANAL SEX WITH WIVES
Is anal sex with one's wife is lawful?

Q: Is a husband permitted to have anal sex with his wife?

A: Having anal sex with one's wife is strictly prohibited by the Holy Qur'an and the Prophetic Sunnah. This is the opinion of both the earlier and later scholars. It is termed as *"Al-Lutiyyah Al-Sughra"* [the lesser sodomy]. It is narrated after the Prophet (peace be upon him) that he said: "Allah does not shy of truth! Do not have anal sex with your wives!" In the Qur'an Allah says what means: **"Your**

**wives are your tilth for you, so go to your tilth, when or
how you will, and send (good deeds, or ask Allah to
bestow upon you pious offspring) for your own selves
beforehand."** (2:223)

According to Islam, man is permitted to have sex with
his wife from any direction, so long as it is in her vagina.
Should he have sex with her in the anus, and she accepts it,
both of them should be given a discretionary punishment.
If they then insist on this, they should be separated from
one anther.

Nushuz [disobedience of the wife]
A woman who fasts during the day and prays during the night and refuses her husband's invitation to the bed

Q: A man has a wife how used to fast all day and observe
prayer during the night and refuses her husband's invitation
to the bed. What is the judgment on this?

A: According to the consensus of Muslim scholars, this is
permitted to her. Rather, she should answer the invitation
of her husband to bed, as this is an obligation on her.
Fasting all day and observing optional night prayer is
something supererogatory. How then can it be given
precedence over the obligation? In a hadith the Prophet

(peace be upon him) said: "A woman cannot observe Fasting in the presence of her husband except after taking his permission."

If supererogatory Fasting of a woman in the presence of her husband in not permitted except after his permission, it is even worse if she refuses his invitation to bed. In the Two Sahihs it is narrated: "If a man invites his wife to bed but she refuses, the angels will curse her until the morning." In the Qur'an Allah says what means: "Therefore the righteous women are devoutly obedient, and guard in (the husband's) absence what Allah would have them guard." (4:34) The right of the husband on his wife comes directly next to the rights of Allah and His Messenger (peace be upon him).

The Prophet (peace be upon him) said: "If I were to order a human being to prostrate to a human being, I would have ordered the wife to prostrate to her husband. This is because he has a great right on her." Once some women said to the Prophet (peace be upon him): Men fight in the cause of Allah, pay charity and do righteous deeds, which we cannot do. He replied: "Observing good matrimonial relationship with the husband equals all these deeds."

*   *   *

DIVORCE AND ANALOGOUS CASES

KHUL' [DEMAND OF DIVORCE MADE BY THE WIFE IN RETURN FOR A

COMPENSATION GIVEN TO THE HUSBAND]

Khul' in the Qur'an and Sunnah

Q: What is Khul' as in the light of the Qur'an and Sunnah?

A: The Khul' mentioned in the Qur'an and Sunnah is the case when a wife hates her husband and wants to separate with him. She in turn repay to the husband the amount of dower or part of it, thus setting herself free from him as a captive is ransomed. If both parties still feel desire to each other, Khul' in this case is innovative and alien to the precepts of Islam. But if the wife really hates her husband and chooses to separate with him, she may ransom herself by repaying the dower to him and absolving him from any liabilities due to her, on the condition that he divorces her by way of Khul'. This is according to the teachings of the Holy Qur'an and Sunnah, as well as the consensus of Muslim scholars.

*   *   *

The forced divorce

Q: A woman who was averse to her husband, asked him to divorce her by way of Khul', threatening that she might commit suicide, should he did not divorce her. Her guardian forced the husband to separate with her. She then married to another husband. The first husband demanded her to return to him because the divorce he made was under coercion. However, she wanted to remain with the second husband. What is the judgment on this case?

A: If the first husband was really forced to separate with her, because of his negligence of his duties towards her, or because he inflicted harm on her without a rightful claim, in word or in deed, the separation will be valid. The second marriage will be valid also and she will be considered the wife of the second husband.

However, if coercion is made by beating the husband or confining him, despite his being good to her, separation will not be valid. Rather, if the wife feels averse to him, despite his being good to her, he may be demanded to separate with her, but not forced to do so. If he complies, it is alright. But if he refuses, the wife will be ordered to be patient, should there be no valid causes that annul marriage.

*   *   *

Accusing the wife of adultery

Q: A man accused his wife of adultery. He based his accusation on the incident that he sent her to attend a wedding, then he spied on her and found out that she was not there. She then denied this incident. When the husband told that to her family, and they asked her to confront him and defend herself, she refused, fearing that he might beat her afterwards. She then went to the house of her maternal uncle. The husband thus made that a proof to cancel all her rights, claiming that she got out from his house without his permission. Is this a rightful claim to slip the wife of her rights?

A: Allah the Almighty says what means: **"O you who believe! You are forbidden to inherit women against their will; and you should not treat them with harshness, that you may take away part of the Mahr you have given them, unless they commit open illegal sexual intercourse; and live with them honorably. If you dislike them, it may be that you dislike a thing and Allah brings through it a great deal of good."** (4:19) It is not lawful for a man to prevent his wife from marrying another husband, in case life between them comes to a deadlock, in order to press her to remit him from the duties he owes her in the instance of divorce.

If the wife, however, commits indecency that is clearly proved, in such case the husband will have the right to prevent her and even beat her.

As for the family of the wife, they should ascertain which of the two parties has the right claim and support him/her in his/her case. If it is found out that the wife is the guilty party, she should ransom herself from him. If the husband claims that he sent her to a wedding, but she went elsewhere, he has the right to ask where she went. If he is told that she went to trustworthy people and those people

witnessed to that, or they admitted that she neither went to
them nor went to the wedding, this is considered a valid
reason to arose the doubt of the husband, and will be
regarded as a support of the husband's claim.

Regarding the trousseau of the wife, she will be
entitled to take it in all circumstances. If both the husband
and wife reconcile, it will be better for them. Whenever
the wife repents, it will be permissible for her husband to
keep her under his custody. There will be no harm in this,
as one who repents from a sin becomes like one who did
not commit any sin. If they could not reach a settlement,
the wife should absolve the husband of the amount of
dower, thus the husband is to separate with her by virtue of
Khul'. Allah the Almighty says what means: **"Then if you
fear that they would not be able to keep the limits
ordained by Allah, then there is no sin on either of them
if she gives back (the Mahr or a part of it) for her Khul'
(divorce)."** (2:229)

*   *   *

The Khul' of a woman who has no guardian

Q: A previously married major woman who had no
guardian except legal authorities, married through legal
authorities, since she had no guardians. The wife then
agreed with her husband to be divorced by way of Khul',
on the condition that she would absolve him of the amount

of dower without taking the permission of her guardian (i.e. legal authorities.) Are Khul' and absolution valid in this case?

A: If she is major enough to make a donation, her Khul' and absolution of dower will be valid, even without the permission of legal authorities.

*   *   *

Cancellation of absolution

Q: A man said to his wife: "If you absolve me of your dower, you will be divorced," thus she absolved him, being not under a legal interdiction, and having no father or brother. She then claimed that she was insane, in order to render the absolution of the husband of the dower void. What is the judgment of this case?

A: Absolution of the dower cannot be rendered void by her mere claim of insanity. Rather, if proof is established that she was insane, but she was not under a legal interdiction, still the absolution of dower cannot be regarded effective, even if she manages her affairs by herself.

*   *   *

Divorce after the absolution of the dower

Q: A woman absolved her husband of all her dower. He then brought witnesses to testify that he divorced her due to absolving him of the amount of dower. Is this divorce valid? Is it revocable or irrevocable?

A: If the husband agrees with the wife to divorce her in return for absolving him of the dower, such divorce will be effective and will be regarded as irrevocable. The same applies if he says to her: "Absolve me of the dower and I will divorce you," or "If you absolve me of the dower, I will divorce you," and suchlike phrases that indicate divorce conditioned by absolution of the dower. However, if she absolves him without the intention of asking for divorce, then he divorces her afterwards, divorce will be revocable.

A question is aroused whether the wife can revoke the absolution of the dower. Usually woman resorts to absolving her husband of the dower either out of her wish to part with him, or for fear of divorce, or that the husband might not marry another woman. In such instances, two narrations reported after Imam Ahmad, one confirming the opinion of revoking the absolution of the dower and one opposing it. If the wife willingly absolves the husband of the dower without any reason, not anticipating any return, in such case she will undoubtedly be entitled to revoke the absolution of the dower.

*   *

Revocable divorce of a deceived husband

Q: A man divorced his wife a revocable divorce. When the witnesses came to testify the divorce, one of them said to the husband: "Say: I divorce her in return for a dirham," when the husband said that, they said to him, "Now she is free. You cannot return to her except after her consent." If he really cannot return to her, can this absolve him of her rights due to his being deceived by the witnesses?

A: If the husband divorced the wife a revocable divorce, then he was prompted by the witnesses to claim that he divorced her in return for a dirham, and he said that, knowing that it was only a confirmation of the first divorce, not making a second divorce, only the first divorce will be countable and will be revocable. If it was claimed that he intended a second divorce, and it was likely that he knew not that a divorce in return for a compensation is irrevocable, his claim is to take precedence, supported by his oath, especially when the context accords to his claim. The normal case is that the witnesses attend after divorce to testify it.

*   *   *

A RULE IN KHUL'

Is a Khul' counted in the three divorce pronouncements?

Q: Is Khul' counted in the three pronouncements of divorce? Is it necessary that it be pronounced with terms and intention other than those of divorce?

A: There is a famous disagreement among scholars on this question. The first opinion, which is attributed to Imam Ahmad and his followers, is that Khul' is an irrevocable separation and an annulment of marriage, not one of the three possible pronouncements of divorce. If the husband makes Khul' for ten times, he can return to her each time with no need for her to marry another man first. This is one of the two opinions of Imam Al-Shafi'i given is this question, which is chosen by a group of his followers. This is also the opinion of the majority of Hadith scholars.

The second opinion: Khul' is an irrevocable divorce which is counted from the three possible pronouncements of divorce. This is the opinion of many earlier scholars.

The opinion of Imam Ibn Taimyyiah:
Ibn Taimyyiah preferred the opinion of Ibn 'Abbas who decided in a case in which a man divorced his wife twice and made Khul' once. He judged that the woman may return to her husband without marrying another man first. Ibrahim bin Sa'd bin Abi Waqqas, when appointed a governor in Yemen, asked Ibn 'Abbas about this question saying that most of the cases of divorce in Yemen are made in return for a compensation given to the husband. Ibn 'Abbas replied that such act was not a divorce, though it was termed divorce by people by mistake.

The condition of wording and intention in Khul'
Khul' and divorce are valid when made in a language other than Arabic, according to the opinion of the majority of scholars. As there is no language other than Arabic that

has the terms for both divorce and Khul', the distinction between the two will be in the compensation given in the case of Khul', not the wording.

The divorce mentioned in the Qur'an is the instance when a man divorces his wife without receiving a compensation from her, in which case divorce will be revocable. As for divorce made in return for a compensation, it is irrevocable. It is not considered as the known divorce, rather it is more like a ransom with which a wife frees herself from her husband. It is not counted in the three pronouncements of divorce, no matter in which terms it is uttered.

Zhihar

What is the meaning of a husband's saying to his wife:
"You are just like my mother or sister"?

Q: What about a husband who said to his wife: "You are just like my mother or sister"?

A: If he means that she is honored and dignified just like his mother or sister, it is permissible to say so. If he intends that she is like his mother or sister as far as marriage is concerned, this is considered as Zhihar. If he continued to live with her as man and wife, he should not have intercourse with her until he performs the due Kaffarah for Zhihar.

*   *   *

Is divorce effected if a husband demanded to consummate marriage with his wife on a certain day but she was not ready on it?

Q: A man concluded a marriage contract and he wanted to consummate his marriage on a certain day, otherwise his wife will be just like his mother or sister. Yet, the wife was not ready on that night. Is this considered as divorce?

A: No divorce is effected in this case according to the four juristic schools. Yet, this act is considered as Zhihar. If he wanted to consummate marriage, he should first make the Kaffarah mentioned in surah Al-Mujadila. He is entitled to emancipate a Muslim slave. If he has not any, he should fast for two consecutive months. If he can not, he should feed sixty poor Muslims.

*

Is it permissible for a man to reconcile with his wife even after he said to her: You are just like my mother as far as marriage is concerned?

Q: A man got angry with his wife and he said to her: You are just like my mother as far as marriage is concerned. Is it permissible for him to reconcile with her?

A: If he reconciled with her, he should perform the Kaffarah of Zhihar. He is entitled to emancipate a Muslim slave. If he has not any, he should fast for two consecutive months. If he can not, he should feed sixty poor Muslims. He should not live with her as man and wife unless he performed Kaffarah.

*

When a man says that his wife is just like his mother during her absence, is she prohibited for him as a wife?

Q: A man said to his friend: Dear brother, it is not desirable to perform such acts before your wife. The other replied: she is just like my mother. His friend said: Why do you say so? I know that she became prohibited for you as a wife once you said so. The man repeated: I swear she is just like my mother. Does she become prohibited for him?

A: All praise be to Allah, the Lord of the Worlds. It all depends on his intention. If he means that she is just like his mother to the extent that she does not blame him for his bad acts or reveals such acts before others, she is not prohibited for him as a wife. Yet he should be punished somehow.

When `Umar bin Al-Khattab (may Allah be pleased with him) heard a man calling his wife: "O sister!", `Umar blamed him for that and punished him somehow. If the man does not know this to be prohibited in Islam, he does not deserve to be punished, although he had performed an ugly deed. A man should not call his wife as his mother.

If he intends that she is just like his mother as far as marriage is concerned i.e. to have intercourse with her and perform such acts only allowed with one's wife, this is considered as Zhihar according to the Juristic schools of Abu Hanifah, Shafi`I and Ahmed.

According to Malik, there is disagreement whether this is considered as a thrice divorce. He should not have intercourse with her unless he performed Kaffarah. He is entitled to emancipate a Muslim slave. If he has not any, he should fast for two consecutive months. If he can not, he should feed sixty poor Muslims. If he performed either, she is no longer prohibited for him.

In conclusion, it is not divorce at all. Yet a man should not have intercourse with his wife in this case unless he performed Kaffarah according to the unanimous agreement of Muslim Imams. Allah knows best.

*   *   *

When a man says to his divorced wife: If I resumed marriage with you, you will be just like my mother, what should he do?

Q: What about a man who said to his divorced wife: If I resumed marriage with you, you will be just like my mother or sister? Is it allowed to resume marriage with her? What should he do?

A: All praise be to Allah, the Lord of the Worlds. According to some scholars, he should perform Kaffarah of Zhihar act. According to others, he is not entitled to perform it. It is safer for a person to adopt the first view.

Divorce

Is a drunkard's divorce effected?

Q: When a drunkard who lost consciousness divorces his wife, is it effected?

A: All praise be to Allah, the Lord of the Worlds. There are two points of view in this case according to scholars. The soundest of which is that a drunkard's divorce is not effected. This is the opinion held by the Emir of the Believers `Uthman bin `Affan and no different opinion was held by any other companion as far as I know.

This opinion was also adopted by many ancient and modern scholars such as `Umar bin `Abdul `Aziz, Imam Ahmed and some of his followers, Imam Shafi`I in an old narration and some of his followers, and some of Abu Hanifah's followers such as Al-Tahawi as well as many others.

I believe that this is the soundest opinion. When Ma`iz bin Malik came to the Prophet (peace be upon him) and confessed that he had committed adultery, the Prophet commanded his companions to smell his mouth in order to check whether he is drunkard or not. If he had been drunkard, his confession would have been considered invalid. It is well known that a drunkard is a sinner because he drank prohibited beverages, but he does not know what he really said during drunkenness.

Deeds are judged according to one's intention while a drunkard never has a straightforward intention. It is the same as if he had a prohibited food or drink which made him mad. Although his madness is caused by committing a sin, his divorce or any other sayings are not valid.

When one studies the principles and goals of the Islamic religion, he comes to judge this opinion as sound and that there is no strong proof to support the opinion that a drunkard's divorce is valid.

Divorce is not valid when made by a person who does not know what he says. If his prayer is not valid because of drunkenness, his divorce is invalid as well as Allah the Almighty said: "Approach not prayers with a mind befogged, until ye can understand all that ye say." Allah knows best.

*   *   *

Is divorce effected when a man who lost his consciousness uttered it?

Q: A man made a stormy quarrel with his wife which made him lose his consciousness. **Then he said to his wife: You are thrice divorced. Is it valid?**

A: All praise be to Allah. If he reached such a state of unawareness that he can not judge what he says, his divorce is not effected. Allah knows best.

If an angry man said: "she is divorced", but he did not mention his wife, is such divorce effected?

Q: If an angry man said: "she is divorced", but he did not mention his wife or her name, is such divorce effected?

A: If he did not intend to divorce her, his divorce is not effected.

*　　*　　*

Is divorce effected when a man is coerced to do it?

Q: What about a man who was coerced to divorce his wife?

A: If a man is unjustly coerced to divorce his wife, his divorce is not effected according to the majority of scholars such as Malik, Shafi`I and Ahmed ... etc. This is the opinion held by the companions of the Prophet (peace be upon him) such as `Umar bin Al-Khattab and others. If a man is surrounded by a group of people who harbor enmity for him and they beat him while he can not defend himself, and he claimed that they coerced him to divorce his wife, his claim is accepted. If there had been witnesses who attest that he had already divorced his wife, but he claims that he had been coerced to do so, his claim is accepted. Asking him to swear is a controversial point among scholars.

*   *   *

If a man is coerced to divorce his wife and he did, but after divorce she got married to another man, is this marriage valid?

Q: A man was imprisoned, beaten and coerced to divorce his wife for the first time. She was pregnant and she married another man. What about this marriage?

A: All praise be to Allah. This divorce is not valid. Her marriage to another man while she is pregnant is invalid according to the unanimous agreement of Muslims. Such marriage is invalid even if she had been divorced. How comes that this happened while she is pregnant and even divorce is not effected? The people who coerced the man and those who conclude the second marriage contract should be punished somehow. The second husband must divorce the woman until her `Iddah (waiting period) from her first husband comes to an end.

As for the `Iddah from the second husband, it is a controversial point among scholars. If the second husband knows that his marriage with her is forbidden, the sound opinion is that there should be an `Iddah. If he thinks that such marriage is valid, there must be an `Iddah from him.

**A man promised his wife to divorce her, but he
had the intention to resume marriage with her
and conclude a new marriage contract with
another dowry, is this valid?**

Q: A man said to his wife: I do not want you. Go to your
family. I am going to divorce you. He really intended to
divorce her. Is it valid to resume marriage with her and
conclude a new marriage contract with another dowry?

A: The promise to divorce is not effected and it is neither
obligatory nor desirable to fulfill it. If he really divorced
her and by saying "Go to your family", he meant divorce,
she is once divorced unless he intended more. He has the
right to resume marriage with her during her waiting
period even without her consent, her custodian or dowry.
Allah knows best.

*   *   *

**Is it permissible for a man to divorce his wife
just because his mother hates her?**

Q: A woman hates the wife of her son although she has
given birth to children. The husband's mother advises him
to divorce her. Is it allowed for him to do so?

197

A: It is not allowed for him to divorce her just because his mother said so. At the same time, he should treat his mother well, but this does not mean that he should divorce his wife. Allah knows best.

* * *

When a mother wants to separate between her daughter and her husband, is the daughter a sinner if she disobeyed her mother in this regard?

Q: When a mother wants to separate between her daughter and her husband although they are in harmony with each other, is the daughter a sinner if she disobeyed her mother in this regard?

A: All praise be to Allah. When a woman gets married, she must not obey her father or her mother in leaving her husband. She must obey her husband unless he ordered her to commit a sin. Obeying him is given priority over her parents.

The Prophet (peace be upon him) said: "If a woman died while her husband is content with her, she will enter Paradise." If the mother wants to separate between them, she belongs to those who sow the seeds of enmity between people. The daughter should not obey her even if her mother invoked Allah against her. Obeying the mother is accepted if her daughter and her husband are performing sins, or if the husband used to order his wife to disobey Allah and His Messenger.

*   *   *

Is divorce effected if the husband intends to divorce his wife before witnesses but he did not utter it?

Q: A man intended to divorce his wife once she menstruated but he did not utter it. When she menstruated, he though that she is divorced and he said to some witnesses: I have divorced her. They inquired: "When?" He said: "The day before yesterday". When two monthly periods passed, other than the period on which he divorced her, the witnesses offered her in marriage to another man. After a period, the second husband also divorced her. When she completed her waiting period, the first husband wanted to marry her again. Is she legal for him as per the first marriage contract? Or is it necessary to make a new contract?

A: If he intends to divorce her once she menstruated, such divorce is not valid according to the unanimous agreement of scholars. He must divorce her actually. If he believes that such intention means divorce, it is not valid but its consequences are taken into consideration. If no divorce is effected, she is still his wife. Allah knows best.

When a man thrice divorces his wife unintentionally and he means just once, is it effected?

Q: A man quarreled with his wife and he wanted to divorce her once, but he erred and he divorced her thrice. What is the legal judgment?

A: All praise be to Allah. If he erred and divorced her thrice while he intends just once, only one divorce is effected. Even if he erred and intended to say another word instead of divorce but he said it unintentionally, no divorce is effected. Allah knows best.

*

A man is indebted to his wife and he wanted to divorce her if he did not pay his debt. If she acquitted him from such debt, is divorce effected?

Q: A man was indebted to his wife who said to him: I am afraid that you may not pay me back. He replied: If I have not settled such debt by the end of Ramadan, you are thrice divorced. The husband is now absent in Qus and he did not appoint an agent to act on behalf of him. If the wife acquitted him, is divorce effected?

A: If she acquitted him, he should not divorce her according to many jurists such as Abu Hanifah, Muhammad, Ahmed and others. If she acquitted him, there is no debt to be settled. The same thing applies when a man pays the debt on behalf of another as the lender obtained his money.

The Prophet (peace be upon him) said to a woman: "If there had been a debt on your mother (or father), would you have paid it? She replied: Yes. The Prophet said: Allah's rights are better fulfilled.

*   *   *

Is it permissible for a man to re-marry his ex-wife whom he divorced thrice before consummating marriage with her?

Q: Is it permissible for a man to re-marry his virgin ex-wife whom he divorced thrice before consummating marriage with her?

A: All praise be to Allah. Divorcing a woman thrice before or after consummating marriage makes her illegal for the husband until she married another who, in turn, divorced her. This is the opinion held by the four juristic schools.

*   *   *

A woman is divorced thrice before consummating marriage and when she gets

married again, she is also divorced thrice from the second husband before the consummation of marriage as well. Is it legal for her to return to the first husband?

Q: A man made a marriage contract but he did not consummate marriage and he divorced his wife thrice. Then she married another man who, in turn, did not consummate marriage and divorced her thrice. Is it permissible for the first husband to return to her?

A: Divorce before the consummation of marriage is just like after consummating it according to the four Juristic Schools. She is not legal for the first husband until she marries another who consummates marriage with her. If the second husband divorces her before consummating marriage, it is not legal for the first.

*   *   *

Does a woman become prohibited for her husband if he said: All that I own is prohibited for me?

Q: A man said: All that I own is prohibited for me. Does his wife become prohibited for him?

A: This is a controversial point among scholars whether it is divorce or Zhihar. Imam Malik believes that this is divorce, but Abu Hanifah and Shafi`I say that he should make a Kaffarah for his oath. Ahmed sees that he should perform a Kaffarah of Zhihar. If he has another intention, this a controversial point. The soundest opinion is that it is not divorce.

*   *   *

When a woman says to her husband: "Divorce me" and he replied: "You are prohibited for me", is she prohibited in this case?

Q: A man made a quarrel with his wife and he beat her. She said to him: "Divorce me" and he replied: "You are prohibited for me". Is she really prohibited?

A: There are two points of view in this case. The first view is that he should perform a Kaffarah of Zhihar if she lets him have intercourse with her. The second view is that he is not entitled to perform anything. Scholars agree unanimously that she must let him have intercourse with her. Allah knows best.

*   *   *

Is it permissible to authorize the new wife to divorce the old one? Is divorce effected?

Q: A man has a wife and children. He married another one and wrote an authorization letter to the effect that if

203

the new wife hated the old one, she has the right to divorce her on his behalf. The term of this authorization letter is ten years. Later, he divorced the authorized woman. Is such authorization valid? Will it be invalid because the authorized woman is divorced?

A: All praise be to Allah. Some may think that this question is related to authorization depending on the fact that if a husband authorized his wife in a sale contract, for example, and later he thrice divorced her, such authorization is not valid as mentioned by jurists. The case here is different.

This authorization letter is invalid once he divorced her, because he did not intend to divorce his first wife. The man's intention was to make the second wife have full freedom in divorcing the first. He means that if the second wife did not want another wife to live with her husband, she has the right to divorce her. Once the authorized woman is divorced, she has no right to use such authorization letter. The husband made such letter just to please his second wife and now she is thrice divorced. It is now meaningless.

As for stipulating certain conditions in the marriage contract such as not to make polygamy, some scholars believe that such conditions are valid. If the husband breached the condition and married another, the wife has the right to terminate the contract. This is a more expressive case than our case here in which he authorized the new wife to divorce the old one once she hated her. In both cases, the authorized woman has the right to act according to the contract or letter when there is already another wife. According to Abu Hanifah and Shafi`I, such conditions are invalid.

The authorization letter is permissible according to the unanimous agreement of Muslim scholars and the authorizer has the right to terminate it. If one said to his wife: "You are free to divorce yourself", this is a controversial point among scholars. According to Ahmed and Shafi`I, it is just an authorization and the husband has the right to terminate it before she uses it. On the other hand, according to Abu Hanifah and Malik, the man does not have the right to terminate it.

According to Ahmed, Malik and other scholars, if the man stipulates that if he married another wife, she would have the right to be divorced so long as she is his wife. Once he divorced her, she does not have any right to such stipulation. Allah knows best.

*   *   *

When a man's authorized agent thrice divorces his (the man's) wife, is it permissible for the husband to return to his wife?

Q: A quarrel occurred between a man and his wife. He was about to travel and he said to his agent: If she is content with this sum of money as her expenses, hand it over to her. If she is discontent, divorce her. After the

205

man's travel, the agent divorced her. When the husband knew what happened, he summoned witnesses and testified that he had decided to return to her and sent for her. When the agent was informed what the husband had done, he informed him that he thrice divorced her. Is it permissible · for the husband to resume his conjugal life after the agent had told him so?

A: All praise be to Allah. The agent should have divorced her once not thrice except with the husband's consent. If the husband told the agent that he did not have the intention to divorce her thrice, his saying is accepted and the agent would not have the right to divorce her thrice. If the agent divorced her once and then her husband returned to her, it is a legal matter. Allah knows best.

*

Is divorce effected when a man is forgetful or when he uttered wrong words?

Q: A man said: My wife is divorced if I continued to swear an oath of divorce unless I had been forgetful. He quarreled with another man and was put in a critical situation, whereupon he said: I swear all oaths according to Malik's Juristic School that I must submit a complaint against you to the ruler. He forgot his former commitment that he will never swear an oath of divorce. He followed the Shafi`I Juristic School. What should he do?

A: If he forgot the first oath and swore a second one, there is no sin on him. Allah knows best.

206

A man said to his wife: You are divorced if I see so-and-so at your house. Is divorce effected if he saw her in another place?

Q: A man said to his wife: You are divorced if I see so-and-so at your house. Is divorce effected if he saw her in another place or if she left the place before his arrival?

A: If she left before his arrival or he saw her with his wife in another place, no divorce is effected. Allah knows best.

＊　　　＊　　　＊

If the wife got out of the house without her husband's permission while he swore an oath that she should not do so, is divorce effected?

Q: A wife got out without her husband's permission. He said to her: You are thrice divorced if you get out of the house without my permission. Is divorce effected immediately or when she gets out? What if he gave her a permission later?

A: She is not to be divorced immediately, but she is divorced once she gets out of the house. If he gave her a

207

general permission to get out, it is permissible for her to get out. Allah knows best.

*　　　　　*

A man accused his wife of stealing a sum of money and said to her: If you did not bring this money, you are divorced. Is divorce effected?

Q: A man accused his wife of stealing a sum of money. She said: I swear by Allah that I have not stolen it. He said: If you did not bring this money, you are thrice divorced. What about the status of the wife?

A: If it turns out that she did not steal the money, she is not to be divorced according to the soundest opinion held by scholars. The husband means that she is divorced only if she had taken the money. Allah knows best.

*　　　*　　　*

When the husband says to his wife: "you are divorced if you give birth to a female baby", and he revoked his threat. The woman gave birth to a female baby. Is divorce effected?

Q: While his wife is pregnant, the husband said to her: "you are divorced if you give birth to a female baby". Before giving birth, he revoked his threat. Later the woman gave birth to a female baby. Is divorce effected?

A: If he divorced her irrevocably or he left her until her `Iddah (waiting period) comes to an end, there are two famous opinions held by scholars in this regard. Imam Shafi`I also held two opinions in this regard; one of them is that divorce is effected, and this is the opinion of Ahmed as well. If he did not revoke his divorce and returned to her during the waiting period, the marriage contract is still valid. Divorce is effected if he left the matter pending (i.e. he still stipulates the condition mentioned in the question.)

*   *   *

During a quarrel with his wife, the husband said: if you say "divorce me", I will do, but she kept silent. What is the legal ruling on this matter?

Q: A man quarreled with his wife and he was hurt. Accordingly, he said: if you say "divorce me", you are thrice divorced, but she kept silent. Then she said to her mother: what does he say? Her mother told her his words. The wife said: Divorce me. Is divorced once or thrice effected?

A: All praise be to Allah. If the husband did not intend that he divorced her at the very same time, he should divorce her before witnesses. If he did not intend anything, he is not a sinner if they left the meeting without divorce. Yet, he should divorce her later as he swore. If he did not intend to divorce her twice or thrice, it is permissible for him to divorce her just once if he wants to fulfill her desire. If she changed her opinion and said: "I do not want to be divorced", he is not a sinner if he did not divorce her. Allah knows best.

*   *   *

If a wife enters a house forgetfully while her husband swears an oath of divorce that if she entered such house, she will be divorced, is divorce effected?

Q: A man said to his wife: "If you enter this house" you are divorced, but she entered forgetfully. Is divorce effected?

A: All praise be to Allah. If he said: "If you enter this house" you are divorced, but she entered forgetfully, no divorce is effected according to the most appropriate opinion held by scholars such as the juristic school of the people of Mecca including `Amro bin Dinar, Ibn Juraij and others. It has also been reported to be one of the opinions of Imam Ahmed. Allah knows best.

Thrice divorce
If a man swore an oath of thrice divorce not to enter his brother's house, but later he was obliged to enter it, is divorce effected?

Q: A man made a quarrel with his brother and swore an oath of thrice divorce not to enter his house, but later he was obliged to enter it, is divorce effected?

A: This is a controversial point of debate among scholars. The strongest argument is that he is not be blamed for such oath and no divorce is effected. Allah knows best.

*   *   *

A man swore an oath of thrice divorce that he will leave the place where he lives. Later, he wanted to return. Is this permissible?

Q: A man swore an oath of thrice divorce that he will leave the place where he lives and he has already left it. Is it permissible to return to it once again?

A: If the reason behind such an oath is non-existent, he can return. Allah knows best.

An angry man swore an oath of thrice divorce that his pregnant wife should not enter her aunt's house. After giving birth, she entered this house. Is divorce effected?

Q: An angry man swore an oath of thrice divorce that his pregnant wife should not enter her aunt's house. After giving birth to a baby, she entered this house. The man once said to other people: If my wife entered her aunt's house after giving birth, she is not to be blamed. Is divorce effected?

A: If the man intends that once his wife gave birth to a child, he is not to be blamed for his oath and that his wife is free to enter her aunt's house, divorce is not effected. Yet his oath is still effective and if his wife entered her aunt's house while she is pregnant, divorce is effected. Allah knows best.

*   *   *

Before his travel, a husband swore an oath of divorce that his wife should not get out of the house during his absence, but out of necessity, she went out. Is divorce effected?

Q: Before his travel, a husband said to his wife: If you get out of the house during my absence, you are divorced. After his arrival, she said to him: There was necessity and I was obliged to get out. Is divorce effected?

A: If she believes that such necessity is not included in his oath and that she does not act in disconformity with his oath when she gets out, divorce is not effected.

*   *   *

When a pregnant woman refuses to have intercourse with her husband and he swore an oath of divorce that he will not have intercourse with her after giving birth. What is the legal judgement if he had intercourse with her after giving birth?

Q: A pregnant woman refused to have intercourse with her husband who was hurt because of such refusal and swore an oath of divorce that he will not have intercourse with her after giving birth. Is divorce effected if he had intercourse with her after giving birth? Is the reason for such an oath taken into consideration?

A: If he had intercourse with her after giving birth, his intention and the reason for such an oath are to be taken into consideration. If he swore this oath · for a certain reason and now this reason is non-existent, no divorce is effected according to the most appropriate opinion held by scholars such as Imam Ahmed and others. If a man swore

213

an oath for a certain reason (for example, not to enter a certain town because its people are unjust but later they became just in their dealing with others, or not to talk to an evil person but later he repented and became straightforward), there are two opinions in this case in Imam Ahmed's Juristic School.

The most appropriate opinion is that he is not to be blamed. Swearing is just like one's commitment to leave a certain act. When a man commits himself not to enter a certain country or not to talk to a man because the country is pagan or the man is an atheist, but later the country embraced Islam and the man became a Muslim, it is permissible to enter it and talk to the man because the reason of commitment is non-existent.

When a man swears not to have intercourse with his wife as a sort of punishing her or because she refuses this matter, but later she became obedient to him, the reason for such an oath is non-existent.

If he intends not to have intercourse with her forever because of her disobedience whether she repented or not, this is another issue. If she properly repented but he intends to punish her as a man will do with his fellow whether he abandoned the sin or not, this also has a different ruling. Allah knows best.

When a man swears an oath of divorce not to have intercourse with his wife for six months, what should he do after the expiry of this period?

Q: When a man swears an oath of divorce not to have intercourse with his wife for six months although she had been previously divorced twice and he intends not to have such intercourse until the period expires, what should he do after its expiry?

A: When the period expires, he has the right to have intercourse with her. He is not a sinner if she did not demand for intercourse after the lapse of four months. This is the opinion held by Malik, Ahmed and Shafi`I and most scholars. This man is called a "Mouli".

*   *   *

Pending Divorce
When a man swears an oath of divorce but he left it pending, is it effected?

Q: When a man swears an oath of divorce but he made it pending, is it effected?

A: No divorce is effected. He is not obliged to perform Kaffarah as well. If he said "Allah willing", no divorce is effected. Allah knows best.

215

When a man says to his wife: "You are thrice divorced" and he has the intention to make it pending, is divorce effected?

Q: A man got angry with his wife and he said to her: "You are thrice divorced". She said: "now", and he replied: "now". He has the intention to make this divorce pending, is it effected?

A: If he intends by saying "I am committed to divorce her" that he does not want to divorce her but that he just urges her to respect him, no divorce is effected. If he said "now, Allah willing", such pending divorce is not effected according to the Juristic Schools of Abu Hanifah and Shafi`i. According to Ahmed and Malik, it is effected as reported by Ibn `Abbas. So long as he intends that divorce is not effected, it is just as a foreigner who speaks some Arabic words which he does not know its meaning.

If a man divorces his wife as a sort of joking, it is effected because he means to divorce her even if he does not intend to put it into effect. The man in question does not mean to divorce his wife and he was not joking as well. This case is just like a man who saw a woman and he said "you are divorced" believing that she is not his wife but it turned to be his wife. In this case also, no divorce is effected according to the most appropriate opinion held by scholars. Allah knows best.

Suraij Question
Is the Suraij Question true?

Q: Is Suraij Question true? If it is not, what about a man who imitated him and acted accordingly? When he knew that it is not true, he repented and asked Allah for forgiveness. Does Allah forgive him?

A: All praise be to Allah, the Lord of the Worlds. This question is a sort of innovation in Islam. None of the Prophet's Companions, their followers or the four Imams adopted it. Some later scholars adopted it, but most Muslim scholars denied it. If a person imitates another as far as this question is concerned and later he repented, Allah will forgive him. He should not divorce his wife even if he married her depending on the interpretation of this question. Allah knows best.

*   *   *

Is it permissible to make a marriage contract in which divorce is stipulated?

Q: A man married a woman and she gave birth to a child. The witnesses advised him that once he consummates marriage with her to say to her: If I divorce you, you are divorced. Is this contract permissible?

217

A: All praise be to Allah. The marriage contract is valid and it should not be made anew. Non-talked "tasrij" does not breach the contract according to the unanimous agreement of scholars. Yet, if he divorced her later, it is effected according to the majority of scholars such as the followers of Malik, Ahmed and Abu Hanifah and many of Shafi`i's followers.

*   *   *

Lineage
If a wife gave birth to a baby after six months of pregnancy, does this baby belong to her husband?

Q: A man married a virgin woman and when he consummated marriage, he checked that she is really virgin. Yet, she gave birth to a baby after six months of pregnancy, does this baby belong to her husband? The husband swore an oath of divorce that the baby belongs to him. Is divorce effected? Please be acknowledged that the baby has no defect as far as his formation is concerned and now he is several years old.

A: All praise be to Allah. If she gave birth to the baby after the lapse of six months, the child belongs to her husband according to the unanimous agreement of Muslim scholars. Such case occurred during the caliphate of `Umar bin Al-Khattab (may Allah be pleased with him).

218

The companions of the Prophet (peace be upon him) found a proof from the Holy Qur'an that the baby could be born after six months of pregnancy as Allah the Almighty said: **"The carrying of the (child) to his weaning is (a period of) thirty months."** and His saying: **"The mothers shall give suck to their offspring for two whole years."** Just as the period of suckling the child is two years out of the thirty months mentioned, the period of pregnancy is six months.

In this verse, Allah mentioned the minimum period of pregnancy and the maximum period of suckling the baby. The child belongs to the husband even if he denied him. How comes that, in this case, he attests that the child belongs to him? Even if he claimed that a fatherless child belongs to him an no other man proclaimed so, the child is his according to the unanimous agreement of Muslim scholars. He is not to be blamed for his oath and no divorced is effected. Allah knows best.

*　　*　　*

Does the baby belong to the first husband if the wife married another man after her waiting period is over?

Q: A man married a woman and he stayed with her for only fifteen days, then he left her after giving a revocable divorce. Later she married another man after telling him that her waiting period is over. The second husband also divorced her after a period of six years. She gave birth to a girl and claimed that she belongs to the first husband. Is such claim true? Please be acknowledged that she and the first husband live in the same town and she did not demand for alimony or expenses for the girl.

A: All praise be to Allah. This girl does not belong to the first husband once she claimed so according to the unanimous agreement of Muslim scholars. Even if she gave birth to the girl when she is divorced and she claimed that the girl belongs to him but he denied so, her claim is not accepted unless she has proved it.

According to Abu Hanifah and one of Ahmed's narraions, a woman is enough as a witness in this regard. According to Malik and the other narration of Ahmed, two women are required. Shafi`I stipulates that there should be four women. As for the man, it is enough if he swore an oath denying that the child belongs to him.

If they are still married and live as man and wife, there are two opinions in Ahmed's Juristic School. The first one is that her claim is not accepted according to Shafi`i's opinion, while the second is that it is accepted according to Malik's opinion. If her waiting period is over and most of her pregnancy period passed, and then she claimed that such fetus belongs to the first husband who divorced her, her claim is not accepted at all according to the unanimous agreement of Muslim scholars. If she said that her waiting period is over and she gave birth to a baby after six months of pregnancy or more, does the baby belong to the husband?

There are two opinions held by scholars in this regard. Ahmed, Abu Hanifah, and Ibn Suraij believe that the child belongs to him. Shafi`i and Malik see that the child does not belong to him. This controversial point is applicable if she did not marry. Yet, if she married after her waiting period is over and then gave birth to a baby after more than six months of pregnancy, it does not belong to the first husband according to the unanimous agreement of Muslim scholars.

As the opinions of the four Juristic Schools are clarified, how comes that the girl belongs to the first husband after the lapse of six years? Even if she said that she had given birth to the girl before he divorced her, her claim is not accepted. His claim is accepted that she does not give birth to the girl during the conjugal period, and he should swear an oath on that. If she said that she gave birth to the girl before she got married to the second husband, while the first denied this, his denial is accepted especially that her claim was very late until she married the second husband. This indicates that she is a liar, in particular according to Malik's juristic school as far as late inexcusable claims are concerned.

*   *   *

A man divorced his wife but a Mufti delivered him a fatwa that divorce is not effected. The man had intercourse with his wife and she gave birth to a child. Was the child born out of adultery?

Q: A man thrice divorced his wife but a Mufti delivered him a fatwa that divorce is not effected. The man adopted his opinion and had intercourse with his wife and she gave birth to a child. Was the child born out of adultery?

A: Whoever claimed so is an ignorant and deviant person who disobeys Allah and His Messenger (peace be upon him). According to the unanimous agreement of Muslims, each marriage contract which the husband believes to be legal and during which the he had intercourse with his wife, the born child belongs to him and they inherit each other. This is also applicable even if the marriage contract is invalid in itself (while the couple does not know), whether the husband is a Muslim or atheist.

When a Jew, for example, marries his niece and she gave birth to a baby, it belongs to him and they inherit each other according to the unanimous agreement of Muslims even if the marriage contract is, in itself, invalid. If one believes that such contract is legal, he is an atheist who must be invited to repent.

Likewise, when an ignorant Muslim marries a woman during her waiting period, as some Bedouins do, and he had intercourse with her, the born child belongs to him and they inherit each other according to the unanimous agreement of Muslims.

*   *   *

The child belongs to the conjugal bed

Confirmation of lineage does not require that the marriage contract be legal. The Prophet (peace be upon him) said: The child belongs to the conjugal bed and the married prostitute is to be stoned till death. When a man thrice divorced his wife but later had intercourse with her believing that divorce is not effected either because of his ignorance, a wrong fatwa delivered by a Mufti, or any other reason, the born child belongs to him and they inherit each other.

The waiting period is to be counted as from the very day on which he ceased from having intercourse with her. If he had intercourse with her believing that she is his wife, she is so and no waiting period is required unless she has been divorced.

*   *   *

Invalid marriage contracts

When a man makes an invalid marriage contract and he had intercourse with his wife thinking that the contract is valid, the born baby belongs to him and they inherit each other according to the unanimous agreement of Muslims. According to the unanimous agreement of Muslim scholars, this case is also applicable if the contract is invalid or there is controversy on its validity.

When a man had intercourse with his wife after divorcing her and this divorce is effected according to the unanimous agreement of Muslim scholars and the marriage contract itself was invalid and the wife gave birth to a baby out of such intercourse, the baby belongs to the husband and they inherit each other. The baby belongs to him because he believes that the marriage is contract is legal and that divorce is not effected because of a wrong fatwa or any other reason. This case is also applicable on invalid contracts according to the unanimous agreement of Muslim scholars. What about the controversial contract?

Even if a man had intercourse with a woman during an invalid marriage such as that made only for pleasure (Mut`ah), or a marriage held without a custodian and witnesses, but he believes it to be legal, the born child belongs to him.

Then what about a controversial marriage although it is proven to be legal according to the Holy Qur'an, the Prophet's Sunnah and analogy?

*   *   *

When a woman gives birth to a baby just two months after the marriage contract although the husband had not consummated marriage with her, is such marriage valid?

Q: A woman gave birth to a baby just two months after the marriage contract is made although the husband had not consummated marriage with her, is such marriage valid? Is he entitled to pay an alimony?

A: All praise be to Allah. According to the unanimous agreement of Muslims the baby does not belong to him and he is not entitled to pay a dowry. Yet, scholars hold tow opinions on the marriage contract:

1. The most appropriate opinion is that it is invalid according to the juristic schools of Malik and Ahmed as well as others. Therefore, marriage must come to an end without paying dowry, as is the case in any other invalid contract. It is rather better if a judge shouldered the responsibility of putting an end to such marriage as a sort of preventing any dispute.
2. The contract is valid but the husband should not consummate marriage until she gives birth. This is the opinion of Abu Hanifah, while Shafi`I believes that he can consummate marriage before giving birth.

If she is pregnant out of a controversial marriage or because the husband had intercourse with her and divorced her before consummating marriage, he should pay half the dowry. If the marriage is invalid according to the unanimous agreement of Muslims, as in this case, he is not entitled to pay dowry if he divorced her before consummating marriage. When a man is coerced to marry a pregnant woman out of adultery, the marriage contract is invalid according to Shafi`I and Ahmed as well as others. If he married her willingly, this is a controversial point among scholars.

Iddah (The Waiting Period)

Is a woman's claim that she no longer menstruates accepted and she gets married according to it?

Q: A woman was divorced on the 28th of Rabi` Al-Awwal and she menstruated once until she was married to another on the 23<sup>rd</sup> of Jumadah Al-Akhirah on the same year. She claimed that she menstruated three times. When the second husband knew that she menstruated only once, he divorced her on the 20<sup>th</sup> of Sha`ban on the same year. She wants to marry the second husband again and she claims that she no longer menstruates. Is her claim accepted? Is it legal to marry her?

A: A woman's claim that she no longer menstruates is not accepted once she said so. If she said so, she is to be left for a year. If she does not menstruate during it, she could be married. If she reached an age where she no longer menstruates, she is not to be left for such year. If she no longer menstruates because of an illness or suckling a baby, she is still in her waiting period until such reason is non-existent.

This woman should have spent two `Iddahs (waiting periods) for each of the two husbands. The second marriage is invalid and hence it does not require that he divorce her. If she menstruated only once and blood ceased continuously, she must spend the two waiting periods after she leaves the second husband. The term of the two waiting periods is six months.

This case is applicable if she no longer menstruates. If she doubts whether she no longer menstruates or not, the waiting periods will be a year and three months. This opinion is based on some jurists' belief that the two waiting periods do not interfere, such as Malik, Shafi`I and Ahmed. According to Abu Hanifah, they interfere but the waiting period of a woman who no longer menstruates is determined if she reached such age.

The opinion which we mentioned is the best and easiest and it was delivered by `Umar bin Al-Khattab. The other opinion that a doubtful woman should stay until she reaches the age when she no longer menstruates is very difficult for people to adopt.

*   *   *

When a judge abrogates a woman's marriage and her husband wants to return to her, is she entitled to a waiting period?

Q: A judge abrogates a woman's marriage after giving birth to a baby because her husband no longer supports her financially for a long period of time. Three months later, he wanted to return to her, is she entitled to a waiting period? It is well known that most women do not menstruate during the period of suckling the baby. Will she wait until the suckling period comes to an end and she menstruates once again?

A: All praise be to Allah. According to the unanimous agreement of the four Juristic Schools and others, she is entitled to a waiting period during which she must menstruate three times even if menstruation did not occur until the suckling period is over.

This is also the judgment of `Uthman bin `Affan and `Ali bin Abi Talib and none of the companions issues a different ruling. If the woman wants to give her baby to another woman to suckle him so that she may menstruate or even she has a medicine for that purpose, it is permissible to do so. Allah knows best.

A woman was divorced after giving birth to six children. After divorce, she did not menstruate for six months. Is it legal for her to marry another man after this period?

Q: A woman used to menstruate when she was a virgin. After her marriage, she gave birth to six children and ceased to menstruate. She was divorced by her husband while suckling her last baby. She stayed with her family for six months and still she did not menstruate. Another man proposed to her. They attended before a judge who asked her about menstruation. She said that she had not menstruated years ago. The judge said: It is not legal for you to marry. Another judge made her marriage contract, but he did not ask her about menstruation. When a third judge was informed of the incident, he summoned the wife and the new husband, lashed him one hundred whips, told him that he had committed adultery and separated between them. The husband did not divorce. Is divorce effected?

A: All·praise be to Allah. If she no longer menstruates because of an illness or because of suckling a baby, she must wait until this reason is non-existent. If she does not know the reason for the cease of menstruation, she should wait for a year and then get married. This is the opinion of `Umar bin Al-Khattab, Ahmed and Shafi`i. Thus her second marriage is invalid. The judge who separates between them is right. If we adopt the other opinion of Shafi`I and a judge made her marriage contract, no other judge has the right to separate between them. Besides, no divorce is effected.

* * *

When a suckling woman has a medicine so that she may menstruate and she has already menstruated thrice, does her waiting period come to an end?

Q: When a divorced suckling woman felt that she did not menstruate a long time ago and she had a medicine so that she may menstruate and she has already menstruated thrice, did her waiting period come to an end?

A: Yes, once she menstruated thrice, it came to an end. If she had a medicine so that she may menstruate and she has already menstruated, it is permissible. If she became hungry or tired and this led to menstruation, and she has already menstruated thrice, her waiting period came to end. Allah knows best.

*   *   *

A sick man divorces his wife but later denied that he had done so. Days later he died. Is the wife entitled to a death or divorce waiting period?

Q: A man got ill for a long time. He ordered his wife to get out of the house but she refused. Accordingly, he said: You are divorced. She got out and veiled herself. When he called her, she entered wearing her veil. When he asked her about the reason for such veil, she told him that he had divorced her. He denied and said that he had not divorced her. Days later, he died. Is she entitled to a death or divorce waiting period?

A: If he was fully aware during divorce, she is entitled to wait for both periods and she has the right to have her due share in his inherited properties. If he was absent-minded

230

and was not aware that he had divorced her, she is entitled to spend the death waiting period. Allah knows best.

*   *   *

Is a woman entitled to spend a death waiting period again if she did not spend it in her house?

Q: A woman used to get out of her house during the death waiting period out of necessity. Is she entitled to spend the waiting period again? Did she commit a sin?

A: Once four months and ten days passed after her husband's death, the waiting period is over and she is not entitled to spend it again. If she was obliged to get out of her house during such period, she is not to be blamed for it. If she went out without any necessity, she should ask Allah for forgiveness and repent to Him, but she is not entitled to spend the waiting period again.

*   *   *

Is it permissible to engage a woman who spent just forty days out of the waiting period of her late husband?

Q: A man died and his wife spent forty days of his death waiting period. Then, she traveled to a faraway town. She

231

did not apply cosmetics or perfumes. Is it permissible to engage her?

A: All praise be to Allah. The death waiting period comes to an end after the lapse of four months and ten days. If there are still some days of this period, she should spend them in her house. She should not get out either at day or night except for a necessity. She should avoid applying cosmetics or perfumes either on her body or clothes. She is allowed to eat whatever food permissible. She can also meet any person permissible for her to meet. If a man proposed to her, she should not give him a clear-cut reply. Allah knows best.

*　　*　　*

If a wife intended to perform pilgrimage with her husband, but he died before travel, is it permissible for her to perform pilgrimage?

Q: If a wife intended to perform pilgrimage with her husband, but he died on Sha`ban, is it permissible for her to perform pilgrimage?

A: according to the unanimous agreement of the four Juristic Schools, it is not permissible for her to travel for pilgrimage during the death waiting period.

Suckling the baby
When two sisters suckle the daughters of each other, is it prohibited for these daughters to marry their cousins?

Q: When two sisters suckle the daughters of each other, is it prohibited for these daughters to marry their cousins?

A: When a woman suckles another's baby five times during the suckling period (the first two years), the (female) baby becomes her daughter. All the children of the suckling woman become brothers and sisters of this suckled baby whether they were born before or after suckling. None of the suckling woman's sons should marry the girl suckled by his mother.

On the contrary, the suckled girl's brothers can marry the daughters of the woman who suckled their sister, provided that such daughters were not suckled by their (the sons') mother. Only the suckled girl is prohibited for the sons of the woman who suckled her.

Thus it is permissible for a man to marry the sister of his sister (by suckling) if he was not suckled by her mother and she was not suckled by his mother. As for the suckled girl, she should not marry any of the sons of the woman who suckled her according to the unanimous agreement of Muslim scholars.

The origin of this case is as follows:

The woman who suckled this daughter becomes her mother. The mother's sons are prohibited to marry this girl and they become her brothers. The woman's brothers and sisters become her uncles and aunts. The woman's husband becomes her father and his brothers and sisters become the girl's uncles and aunts. The suckled girl becomes the daughter of the suckling woman who, in turn, becomes the grandmother of this girls' children after her marriage. As for the suckled girl's brothers, sisters, and parents, they are not affected by suckling according to the unanimous agreement of the four Juristic Schools.

*　　*　　*

Two men were suckled by the same woman, then one of them got married and he had a girl. Is it permissible for the other man to marry this girl?

Q: Two men were suckled by the same woman, then one of them got married and he had a girl. Is it permissible for the other man to marry this girl?

A: When a baby is suckled five times during the first two years by a woman, she becomes his mother. All her children, born before or after suckling him, are his brothers. Suckling prohibits what birth prohibits as regards marriage according to the Sunnah of the Prophet (peace be upon him) and the unanimous agreement of Muslim

234

scholars. Therefore, this man is not allowed to marry the other's daughter just as he is not allowed to marry his brother's daughter.

*   *   *

When a girl is suckled with her cousin, is it permissible for him to marry her sister?

Q: A man has two female cousins; one of them was suckled with him while the second was not. Is it permissible for him to marry the girl who was not suckled with him?

A: When a baby is suckled five times during the first two years by a woman, she is his mother and it is prohibited for him to marry any of her daughters born before or after he had been suckled, because they are his sister according to the unanimous agreement of Muslim scholars.

If a girl was suckled by a woman, she is not allowed to marry any of her sons. If the fiancé was not suckled by the mother of his fiancée neither was she suckled by his mother, it is permissible for them to marry each other according to the unanimous agreement of Muslim scholars. Allah knows best.

Is it permissible for the son of a suckling woman to marry the daughter of the girl who was suckled by his mother?

Q: A woman hired another suckling woman in order to suckle her daughter for a day or month. Is it permissible for the suckling woman's son to marry this girl?

A: All praise be to Allah. If the girl was suckled five times during the first two years, the suckling woman becomes her mother and it is prohibited for her to get married to any of her sons born before or after she had been suckled according to the unanimous agreement of Muslim scholars.

If anyone considers this to be permissible, he is to be invited for repentance. If he does not repent, he is to be killed. If this suckled girl has sisters from her mother, it is permissible for them to get married to any of the suckling woman's sons according to the unanimous agreement of Muslim scholars. Allah knows best.

*   *   *

A man married two wives and a baby was suckled by one of them. This man had a daughter born by the second wife. Now, is it permissible for the suckled person to marry this daughter? If they have already got married, is it permissible for the judge to separate between them?

Q: A man married two wives, one after the other, and a baby was suckled by the first. This man had a daughter born by the second wife. Is it permissible for the suckled person to marry this daughter? If they have already got married, is it permissible for the judge to separate between them? Is this a controversial point among scholars?

A: If the baby was suckled five times during the first two years, he is not allowed to marry this girl according to the unanimous agreement of Muslim scholars.

Ibn `Abbas was asked about a man who had two wives; the first suckles a boy while the second suckled a girl, is it permissible for them to marry each other? He replied: No it is not. Besides, Al-Bukhari and Muslim reported that `A'ishah said: "Aflah, brother of Abu Al-Qu`ais, asked for permission to enter my house. When I was a baby, the wife of Al-Qu`ais suckled me. She said: I shall never permit you until I ask the Prophet (peace be upon him). When she asked him, he said: He is your uncle. Give him permission to enter. Suckling makes prohibited what birth does." If this person mentioned in the question married this girl, the judge should separate between them according to the unanimous agreement of Muslim scholars. Allah knows best.

*   *   *

If a man was not suckled by the mother of a girl neither was she suckled by his mother, but their younger brothers and sisters exchanged suckling

from both mothers, is it prohibited for this man to marry this girl?

Q: If a man was not suckled by the mother of a girl neither was she suckled by his mother, but their younger brothers and sisters exchanged suckling from both mothers, is it prohibited for this man to marry this girl? If he married her and she gave birth to a baby, what is the legal judgment? What is the scholars' opinions in this regard?

A: All praise be to Allah. If the man was not suckled by her mother neither was she suckled by his mother, but his brothers and sisters were suckled by her mother and her brothers and sisters were suckled by his mother, it is permissible for him to marry her according to the unanimous agreement of Muslim scholars. She is considered as the sister of his brother from his father.

Suckling leads to prohibiting some kinds of marriages as far as the suckled person and his offspring, the suckling woman and her husband are concerned. The suckling woman becomes the suckled person's mother, her sons become his brothers whether born before or after he had been suckled, her husband becomes his father, and this husband's sons become his brothers whether born before or after he had been suckled. As for the suckled person's real parents, brothers and sisters, they are marriageable to his suckling mother, her husband and their children.

This opinion is delivered according to the unanimous agreement of Muslim scholars, the four Juristic Schools, the companions and their followers. Some scholars adopt a different opinion that such suckled milk does not lead to prohibiting certain kinds of marriages, but traditions support the opinion of the Muslim scholars.

*　　*　　*

When one of two sisters is suckled with a boy, is it permissible for him to marry the second sister?

Q: There are two sisters; one of them has two daughters and the other has a son. One of these daughters was suckled with this son. Is it permissible for him to marry the second sister?

A: If one of the daughters was suckled by the mother of the son while he was not suckled by her mother, it is permissible for him to marry her sister according to the unanimous agreement of Muslim scholars.

*　　*　　*

When a boy is suckled with a girl, is it permissible for his brother to marry her sister?

Q: A woman left her daughter with the wife of her brother. Upon her return, she asked: Have you suckled her? She replied: "No" and swore that she had not. Her nephew as well as her daughter became old. Is it permissible for them to get married although the nephew has a brother who was suckled with the daughter's other sister?

A: If the daughter was not suckled by the mother's fiancé neither the fiancée was suckled by the daughter's, it is permissible for them to marry each other even if the fiancée's brothers and sisters are her brothers and sisters by suckling.

There is a unanimous agreement among Muslim scholars in this regard. When a baby is suckled by a women, she becomes his mother, her husband is his father and her children are his brothers and sisters. As for his real father, mother, brothers and sisters, it is permissible for any of them to marry any of his brothers or sisters by suckling, as it is permissible for a maternal sister to marry a paternal brother according to the unanimous agreement of Muslim scholars. Allah knows best.

*　　*　　*

When a girl is suckled by her aunt, is it permissible for the aunt's grandson to marry this girl?

Q: A married woman used to have milk in her breasts without giving birth or being pregnant and she suckled her

niece five times during the first two years of her life. Is it
permissible for this aunt's grandson to marry this girl?

A: When a woman is married and she had intercourse with
her husband and there has been milk in her breasts,
suckling this milk leads to prohibiting some sorts of
marriages. When a girl is suckled five time from this
woman, she becomes her mother and this aunt's grandson
becomes the girls nephew and she is his aunt as well
whether she was suckled with him or not. It is permissible
for this grandson to marry the sister of this girl because
she was not suckled by his grandmother.

If a woman who never gets married has milk in her
breasts, suckling it leads to prohibiting some sorts of
marriages according to Abu Hanifah, Malik Shafi`I and a
narration by Ahmed. Yet, Ahmed's doctrine stipulates that
it does not lead to prohibition. Allah knows best.

When a mother denied that she suckled a girl married by her son, is it permissible to separate between them?

Q: A man engaged one of his relatives but her father said
to him: "she was suckled with you", and he refused to let
him marry her. When the father died, he married her.
Witnesses attest that the mother suckled him but later she

denied so and said: I have said so for a certain purpose. Was it permissible for the man to marry her?

A: If the mother was known for telling the truth and that she really suckled him five times, they should be separated if they had already married. This is the soundest opinion held by Muslim scholars. Imam Al-Bukhari reported: The Prophet (peace be upon him) ordered `Uqbah bin Al-Harith to divorce his wife when a black maiden mentioned that she suckled him and his wife.

If it is doubtful whether she tells the truth or not or there is doubt regarding how many times he was suckled, this is a dubious point which should be avoided. They are not to be separated without a strong proof which necessitates such separation.

If the woman denied her saying before they got married, the wife is not prohibited for him. Yet, if it turns out that she was a liar in such denial and that she denied her saying for a certain purpose, it is not permissible for them to get married. Allah knows best.

*   *   *

After a man got married and had many children, he was told that his wife was suckled by his mother. What is the legal judgment on this matter?

Q: After a man got married and had many children, he was told that his wife was suckled by his mother. What is the legal judgment on this matter?

A: If the man who told him so is known for telling the truth and he knows full well what happened, and he said that the wife was suckled by the husband's mother five times during the first two years, his saying is accepted. If he is not a truthful person, he saying is rejected. Allah knows best.

*   *   *

If a man was suckled by a woman when he was a baby and this woman has daughters younger than him, is it permissible for him to marry any of them?

Q: If a man was suckled by a woman when he was a baby and this woman has daughters younger than him, is it permissible for him to marry any of them?

A: If he was suckled by this woman five times during the first two years, he becomes a son of this woman. All children born after or before suckling him become his brothers and sisters according to the unanimous agreement of Muslim scholars.

243

Is it permissible for a man to marry a girl who was suckled with his brother?

Q: A woman has a boy while her sister has a girl. The girl was suckled by the boy's mother, but the reverse did not happen. Later, the boy's mother gave birth to several girls while the girl's mother gave birth to several boys. Is it permissible for one of the boy's brothers to marry the girl who was suckled with his brother? Is it permissible for any of the others boys to marry any of the other girls?

A: All praise be to Allah. It is not permissible for the suckled girl to marry any of the boys of the woman who suckled her whether before or after suckling her. As for the girl's brothers, they can marry any of this woman's daughters and vice versa. Any brother not suckled by this woman can marry any of her daughters. The suckled girl's brothers could marry any of the boy's sisters as long as none of them was suckled by the boy's mother. Prohibition of marriage, in this case, is only restricted to the suckled person. He should not marry any of the daughters of the woman who suckled him. As for his brothers, they can marry any of these daughters. Allah knows best.

A man used his wife's milk in washing his eyes and another suckled milk from his wife. Do their wives become prohibited?

Q: A man's eyes caused him pain and he washed them by using his wife's milk. Does she become prohibited if he drank such milk and it reached his stomach? Another man loves his wife and while flirting her, he suckled some of her milk, does she become prohibited for him?

A: All praise be to Allah. It is permissible for the man to wash his eyes by using his wife's milk and she is not prohibited for him as a wife for the following reasons:

1. He is an old man and if an old man suckled his wife's milk or any other woman's, it does not lead to prohibiting any sort of marriages according to the unanimous agreement of the four Juristic Schools and almost all scholars, as indicated by the Qur'an and Sunnah. `A'ishah's Hadith on Salim, the freed slave of Abu Hudhaifah, is a special case because he adopted him before adoption was prohibited.

2. Washing the eyes with milk does not lead to prohibiting any sort of marriage. This is a point of agreement among all scholars. Yet, there is dispute among scholars when milk is entered through his nose. This leads to the said prohibition according to Abu Hanifah, Malik and one of the narrations of Shafi`I and Ahmed. Most scholars believe that when milk is entered through the nose via means other than suckling, it leads to the

said prohibition. This is also the most renowned opinion in Ahmed's juristic school.

As for the second question, suckling the wife's milk does not lead to the said prohibition according to the unanimous agreement of the four Juristic Schools.

*   *   *

A boy was suckled by a woman, and ten years later, she gave birth to a girl, is it permissible for him to marry this girl?

Q: A boy was suckled by a woman twice, and ten years later she gave birth to a girl, is it permissible for him to marry this girl?

A: If he was suckled five times during the first two years of his life, he becomes her son. It is prohibited for him to marry any of her daughters whether born before or after he had been suckled according to the unanimous agreement of Muslim scholars.

 A "suckling" is defined as the baby's sucking milk from the woman's breasts and then leaving it. If he did so five times in just one suckling, this is considered as five sucklings. The same thing is applicable if he did it in two sucklings. A "suckling" does not refer to the quantity of milk a baby may have each suckling session, because she may suckle him in the morning and evening and during

246

each session, he may have taken many sucklings. Allah knows best.

*　　*　　*

16. When a boy is suckled by a girl's mother and later this boy died, is it permissible for his brother to marry this girl?

Q: A woman has a boy and another has a girl. The girl's mother suckled the boy many times, and later this boy died, is it permissible for his brother to marry this girl? Please be acknowledged that this brother was not suckled by the girl's mother at all.

A: According to the unanimous agreement of the four Juristic Schools, it is permissible for the brother of the suckled boy to marry the daughter of the suckling woman whether the suckled boy is dead or alive. Allah knows best.

*　　*　　*

A boy was suckled by the wife of his uncle when he was more than two years old, is it permissible for him to marry her daughter?

Q: A boy was suckled by the wife of his uncle when he was more than two years old, is it permissible for him to marry her daughter?

247

A: If he was suckled after he had been more than two years old, it is permissible for him to marry her.

* * *

When a woman keeps her breast away from a baby once he starts suckling, is it permissible for him, once he is old, to marry this woman's daughter?

Q: A woman has given another her baby while they were in a public bathroom. The baby starts suckling the woman's breasts while the woman was unaware. She kept away from him and she is not sure whether he had been suckled or not. Is it prohibited for this boy to marry any of the suckling woman's daughters?

A: According to the unanimous agreement of the four Juristic Schools, it is not prohibited for this boy to marry any of her daughters, because she is not his mother and she is not to be prohibited depending on a doubtful event.

* * *

Alimony
A man divorced his wife thrice and he has a girl who is still suckled, is he entitled to pay alimony?

Q: A man divorced his wife thrice and he has a girl who is still suckled, and her family obliged him to pay alimony. What is the term of `Iddah (waiting period) during which she will not menstruate so that she may suckle the girl?

A: All praise be to Allah. According to the majority of Muslim scholars such as Malik, Shafi`I and Ahmed, the woman thrice divorced does not deserve alimony. Abu Hanifah believes that she deserves it so long as she is still in her waiting period. If she still menstruates, her waiting period extends until she menstruates three times. Almost always the woman who suckles is exposed to late menstruation. According to the unanimous agreement of Muslim scholars, she must receive money in return of suckling the girl as Allah said: "And if they suckle your (offspring), give them their recompense." The alimony is to be paid by the well to do while the poor are not entitled to pay it.

*   *   *

When a woman needs money, does she take it from her husband or from her dowry?

Q: When a married woman needs money, does she take it from her husband or from her dowry?

A: A husband is obliged to support his wife financially out of his own money, and not from her dowry. As for the postponed portion of her dowry, it is permissible for her to demand for it. If the husband gave it to her, it is rather better. If he refused, he should not be obliged to do so until they are separated either by death or divorce. Allah knows best.

*   *   *

When a woman disobeys her husband, is he still entitled to support her with money and clothes?

Q: A man married a woman who disobeys him and even though demands for money and clothes, does she deserve them?

A: If she refused to have intercourse with him or she got out of his house without his permission, she does not deserve financial support or clothes. The same ruling applies when he asks her to travel with him but she refuses. As long as she disobeys him, she does not deserve financial support or clothes.

*   *   *

When a man leaves his wife for a whole year and does not support her with money, is it permissible for her to marry another man to support her?

Q: A man married a woman and traveled for a whole year leaving no money to support her. Besides, she does not have any other money to support her and she was about to die out of hunger. A man engaged her and married her. When she became pregnant, the judge was informed of this new marriage and he separated between them. Later, she gave birth to a baby and the second husband kept on supporting her until the boy was four years old. Until now, the first husband did not return and it is not known where he lives. Is it permissible for her to return to the second husband or wait for the first?

A: If the first husband did not support her, marriage could be abrogated. When her waiting period is over, she can marry any other man. Only the judge has the right to abrogate this marriage. If she did it herself for whatever reason, this is a controversial point of disagreement among scholars.

If the judge did not abrogate the first marriage contract and declared that her husband is dead and she married another, such marriage is invalid. If the second husband thinks that this marriage is valid because of the first husband's death or whatever reason, the born baby belongs to him and he should pay her dowry. Yet she must spend a waiting period as the first marriage is abrogated, then she is free to marry whomever she wants.

After a man had married a woman, he left her for a whole year and traveled to his country. He did not send her money, is it permissible for the wife's father to abrogate the marriage?

Q: After a man had married a woman, he wanted to travel to his country. The agent of his father-in-law said to him: "Do not travel. Either you give the advance portion of the dowry and take your wife with you or settle the matter with your father-in-law." He traveled and did not pay attention to the agent's request. He was away for a year and he did not send her money to support her. Is it permissible for the wife's father to demand for abrogating the marriage?

A: Yes it is. Once this husband married her, it is obligatory to support his wife. If he did not, the wife has the right to demand for abrogating the marriage.

*   *   *

When a wife travels with her father without her husband's permission, what is the legal ruling concerning them?

Q: A man married a woman and he supports her financially. Yet, she disobeyed him and even traveled with her father without the husband's permission. What is the legal ruling concerning them?

A: All praise be to Allah. If the father-in-law traveled with the wife without the husband's permission, he is to be punished some way or other. The wife is to be punished as well if she has the ability to refuse such travel. Once she traveled, she does not have the least right to receive financial support from her husband. Allah knows best.

*   *   *

A wife's family asked the husband to provide her with the clothes sufficient for a year and they have already obtained them. Then they demanded for money and said that they will support her. Is this act permissible?

Q: A man married a woman for a year and then a quarrel took place between him and her family. They demanded for the clothes sufficient for a year and they have already obtained them. Then they demanded for money and said that they will support her claiming that they have not allowed him to support her! Is this act permissible?

A: All praise be to Allah, the Lord of the Worlds. If the husband married her according to the legal code and he used to support her with food as it is common with all people, neither she nor her father has the right to demand for financial support.

This was the custom of the Prophet (peace be upon him), his companions and all Muslims in each and every time and this is the ruling delivered by all scholars. If a person charged the husband to give his father-in-law a sum of money in order to buy food for his daughter, he has thus acted in disconformity with the Sunnah of the Prophet (peace be upon him) and the practice of the Muslims, even if some people adopted this opinion.

Yet, in this case, the husband supported her as her father himself confessed. Their demand for money and their claim that the husband's support is not taken into consideration are invalid claims according to the revered Shari`ah. If a man believes that supporting the woman is just like the debt which must be received by her father, he is wrong due to the following:

Supporting a woman means providing her with food and the necessities of life, not saving money for her.

a. The father's reception of such money is a useless act.
b. Demanding for such money does not require the husband's permission, because he is obliged to support her according to the legal code. If her father prevented him from supporting her, his saying is not taken into consideration.
c. Such case depends on the prevalent custom which supports the husband in this regard.

It is not to be claimed that the father has not asked the husband to support her for the following two reasons:

1. The husband is responsible for her according to the legal code and he is to provide her with all her rights such as her physical needs, allotting a day for her in case he married other women and any other rights. According to the Holy Qur'an and Sunnah, men are guardians and supporters of women and women are to be cared for and protected by men.
2. The prevalent custom followed by people in this case supports the husband. Allah knows best.

*   *   *

When a man is imprisoned because he did not settle his wife's financial support and provide her with the necessary clothes, is it permissible for her to demand for support during his imprisonment?

Q: When a man is imprisoned because he did not settle his wife's financial support and provide her with the necessary clothes, is it permissible for her to demand for support during his imprisonment?

A: If he was insolvent and she imprisoned him, she is unjust and she thus denied him his rights entitled on her. During the period of his imprisonment, she does not deserve financial support.

Yet, if he was able to support her and he refrained from giving her due rights after she demanded for them, he is an unjust husband. If she did not refrain from his rights entitled on her, she must have her due financial support.

*　　*　　*

If a wife was of no avail to her husband for two years because of her illness, does she deserve financial support?

Q: If a wife was of no avail to her husband for two years because of her illness, does she deserve financial support? If she does not deserve and a judge issued a legal ruling that she is entitled to have financial support, is the husband obliged to pay it?
A: Yes, she deserves support according to the unanimous agreement of the four Juristic Schools.

*　　*　　*

When a man divorces his wife while she is pregnant, but later she was aborted, does she deserve alimony?

Q: When a man divorces his wife while she is pregnant, but later she was aborted, does she deserve alimony?

A: If she was aborted and thus her waiting period is over, she does not deserve alimony whether the fetus had been body and soul or not, provided that he had been fully created as a human being. If he had not been fully created, this is a controversial point of disagreement among scholars.

*   *   *

Is the husband entitled to pay the waiting period alimony to his wife if she did not spend it at the place he had determined for this purpose?

Q: A man divorced his wife thrice and he ordered her to spend the waiting period at her house, but she left it before the waiting period is over. The husband asked about her and checked that she left the house. Does she deserve the waiting period alimony?

A: She does not deserve such alimony neither has she the right to demand for it on the past period according to the unanimous agreement of the four Juristic Schools. Allah knows best.

Is it permissible for the husband to ask his wife to give him the cost of supporting her child who belongs to a former husband?

Q: A man married a woman who had a child from a former husband. His father supports him with money which the wife receives. The current husband used to support the child for years. When he married, there had been an amount of five Dinars as a portion of the dowry to be paid to the wife at that time. The wife stipulated that she would not demand for such money as long as he supports her child. She did not appoint a certain sum of money as a financial support to the child. Is it permissible for the husband to ask his wife for the cost of supporting her child during the period the child lived with him?

A: If he did not fulfill the condition which his wife stipulated, he does not have the right to demand for the cost of supporting the child once he did so willingly. He does not volunteer such money whether he supported the child as per his mother's permission or not.

*　　*　　*

Is a rich son entitled to support his old father, his wife and brothers?

Q: A man became incapable of earning his living and he does not have money to support him. He has a wife and children. Is his rich son entitled to support him, his wife and young brothers?

A: All praise be to Allah, the Lord of the Worlds. Yes, a rich son is entitled to support his father, his wife and his younger brothers. If he did not do so, he has disobeyed his father and severed relations with him and he deserves the penalty of Allah in this world and the Hereafter. Allah knows best.

*　　*　　*

Is it permissible to give one's relatives out of one's Zakah and Kaffarah? What is the legal ruling on giving charity to needy relatives?

Q: What is the legal ruling on giving charity to needy relatives?

A: If one's money is not sufficient to support his relatives and non-relatives, he is obliged to support his relatives first and he should not give charity to non-relatives while his relatives need it. As for Zakah and Kaffarah, it is permissible to give relatives out of them, provided that he is not entitled to support them such as his wife ... etc. If relatives and non-relatives are equally poor, it is rather better to give them to one's relatives.

*　　*　　*

Nursing the baby
Who is to nurse the baby? When is it permissible for the nursing mother to demand for financial support?

Q: A man married a woman and he died leaving an eight-year-old child. The man's father is still alive. The wife asks her father-in-law to support her. Then the wife got married and was divorced. Her father-in-law did not know about this marriage. Later, she took the child and traveled, while his grandfather does not know. Is he entitled to support her with money?

A: Once the mother got married, she does not have the right to nurse the child. If she left her town and traveled, the grandfather has the right to take the child. This woman does not deserve to nurse the child and if she demanded for alimony, she does not have the right to obtain it. If the grandfather is insolvent, he   is not entitled to support his grandson.

*

When a mother takes her child and agrees with her former husband that she will support their child, but later she demanded for financial support, is it permissible?

Q: A   man has a seven-year-old child and his former wife married another man. The man took the child under his custody according to the rulings of the revered Shari`ah and because there is no other supporter for him. His former wife decided to take the child under her custody for a certain period. The man is afraid that once he did so, his former wife may demand for financial support and clothes. Is it permissible for her to demand for them? If they agreed that the mother will take the child while the father will pay nothing, is this permissible?

A: All praise be to Allah, the Lord of the Worlds. So long as she took the child and she supports him and agreed with her former husband on this matter, she does not have the right to demand for financial support according to the unanimous agreement of Muslim scholars. Yet, if she wants to demand for financial support in the future, the father has the right to take the child back and she is not to take him under her custody. If they agreed that she would have the child and support him, is such an agreement binding? This is a controversial point among scholars. According to Malik, it is binding. Therefore, it is permissible to make such agreement. Allah knows best.

*   *   *

Is it permissible for a father to oblige his son to travel oversees without the son's or mother's consent?

Q: A man has a son who traveled oversees to care for his father's trade. He has another son in his teens and his mother is divorced. This son lives with his maternal grandparents. His father wants him to travel in the company of his elder brother. Yet, the son and his mother do not agree to such voyage. Is it permissible for the father to oblige his son to travel?

A: The son is to choose whether to live with his father or his mother. If he chose to stay with his unmarried mother, he has the right to do so and the father can not oblige him to   travel. Yet, he should go to his father during the day in order to teach him and return to his mother at night. If he chose to live with his father, he has the right to do so. If he decided to stay with his father and the father saw that he   should travel, and there is no harm to travel, the father has the right to order him to travel. Allah knows best.

*   *   *

Does the stepfather have the right to put the daughter of his wife from another husband under his custody?

Q: A man married a woman who was formerly married and   has a daughter. The wife died and the girl stayed with her stepfather until he brought her up. A soldier wanted to take the girl under his custody. Is this act permissible?

A: This soldier does not have the right to put her under his custody. If there is none of her relatives to put her under his custody, the most suitable person should take her under his custody. It is prohibited for her stepfather to marry her while the case is not so with the soldier. If her stepfather takes proper care of her, she should not go to another person considered as stranger for her and it is not permissible for him to look at her and stay alone with her.

*

What about the son put under the custody of his mother?

Q: What about the son put under the custody of his mother?

A: When a son is put under his mother's custody and she spent money on him hoping that she will ask her former husband to repay it, she has the right to do so. This is the opinion of Malik and Ahmed. They believe that when a person does something on behalf of another, such as settling his debt or supporting his slaves, he should return such money even if the person who did so has not asked for the other's permission. Allah, the Almighty, said: "And if they suckle your (offspring), give them their recompense."

Allah ordered the husband to give the mother due recompense for nursing the baby. Allah did not mention any conditions or agreements in this regard. If she volunteered to take the child under her custody, she does not have the right to ask her former husband for support.
If the man stipulated that if she traveled with the child to another city, she would not have financial support, he has full right to do so, even if she intends to return back. She is not entitled to travel without his father's permission and

263

if she traveled, she has caused him injustice. Allah knows best.

*   *   *

Clarification and Comment

The mother is the most suitable person to take the child under her custody.

What will happen if an event occurred which prevented the mother from taking the child under her custody? The mother may not fulfill one of the conditions required as far as custodianship is concerned. She may even die. In this case, another custodian should take care of the child according to the order ranked by Shari`ah as follows:

The mother -maternal grandmother –paternal grandmother – full sister – maternal sister – paternal sister – niece (daughter of a full sister) – niece (daughter of a maternal sister) --mother's aunt –father's aunt –paternal sister's niece - full sister's niece - maternal brother's niece - paternal brother's niece – full aunt (father's sister) – paternal aunt – mother's maternal aunt – father's maternal aunt - mother's paternal aunt - father's paternal aunt - The full aunt is given priority in the last two cases.

If the child has none of the female relatives mentioned above, or if none of them is apt to take him under her

264

custody, custodianship is moved to the men non-marriageable to the female child. Order is ranked according to their right in inheritance as follows:

The father – grandfather – full brother – paternal brother – nephew (of a full brother) – nephew (of a paternal brother) – full uncle – paternal uncle – the full uncle of his father – the paternal uncle of his father.

If there is none of the child's male relatives or none of them is apt to take him under his custody, the right of custodianship moves to those men of his relatives through the mother as follows:

The grandfather – brother – nephew (of a maternal brother) – the uncle of his mother – maternal uncle – full uncle – paternal uncle – maternal uncle.

If the child has no relatives, the judge should appoint a custodian to bring him up.

*   *   *

Crimes and Penalties
Unintentional and premeditated murder

Q: Is the unintentional or premeditated murderer entitled to the Kaffarah mentioned in the Holy Qur'an "a fast for two months running"? Or is he entitled to pay the blood money?

A: Unintentional murder entitles its doer to pay blood money and perform Kaffarah, and he is not a sinner.

Premeditated murderer is a sinner, and even if the murdered person's family forgave him or took the blood money, the murdered person's rights are not absolved in the Hereafter. If the family of the murdered killed the murderer, this is a controversial point in Ahmed's juristic school. The soundest opinion is that such right is not absolved. If the murderer's good deeds are so many, some of them may be taken so as to please the murdered, or Allah may compensate him if the murderer sincerely repented.

An unintentional murderer is entitled to pay the blood money according to the Holy Qur'an and the unanimous agreement of Muslim scholars. Blood money is to be paid if the murdered is a Muslim or one of the People of the Book as the Holy Qur'an indicated and as declared by the Muslim scholars and Imams. There is no old controversy on this matter. Yet, some recent scholars of Al-Zhahiriah claim that if the murdered belongs to the People of the Book, no blood money is to be paid.

As for the premeditated murderer, he must be put to death in return. Yet, if he agreed with the murdered person's family on a blood money, this is a permissible act according to the Holy Qur'an and the unanimous agreement of Muslim scholars. Such blood money is to be paid out of the murderer's money, in contrast with the unintentional murderer who can pay the blood money out of his family's money.

As for Kaffarah, the majority of scholars say that premeditated murder, just like perjury and adultery, is too heinous to be compensated. This is the opinion of Malik,

Abu Hanifah and Ahmed. Kaffarah is to be performed in case a man had said to his wife: "you are just like my mother or sister" and then had intercourse with her or a man had intercourse with his wife during a Ramadan day. In another narration, Shafi`I and Ahmed say that Kaffarah is obligatory in case of premeditated murder and perjury, and they agree that a man is not absolved of the sin once he performed Kaffarah.

*   *   *

When a group of people conspired to murder a person but just one of them performed the plot, will they be killed all or just the murderer?

Q: A group of people conspired to murder a person but just two of them attended the act. Will they be killed all or just the murderer?

A: All praise be to Allah. If there is a clear-cut proof that a certain person (or more) murdered him, he (they) would be murdered in return by the family of the murdered person. This family has the right to murder only some of them. If a certain murderer was not defined, the family of the murdered would swear on one of this group that he had performed the plot and he is to be murdered accordingly. Allah knows best.

When a man beats another and later the beaten person falls dead, what is the legal judgment in this case?

Q: A man beats another and later the beaten person fell dead. Between being beaten and his death, the man was very weak because of such beating. What is the legal judgment in this case?

A: All praise be to Allah, the Lord of the Worlds. If the aggressor beats him out of enmity, this is a semi-premeditated murder. Therefore, the aggressor should pay an exorbitant blood money, but he is not to be murdered in retaliation. This ruling is applicable if his death does not result from such beating.

*   *   *

The penalty of adultery
If the adulterer repented before due penalty is afflicted, is penalty canceled?

Q: When an adulterer repents before due penalty is afflicted, is penalty canceled?

A: When a person repented from committing adultery, robbery or drinking wine before he is referred to the ruler, his penalty is canceled as is the case with the rebels who repent before they are referred to the ruler. This ruling is delivered according to the unanimous agreement of Muslim scholars.

*   *   *

Do the viciousness of sins and the penalty of adultery increase in the blessed days?

Q: Do the viciousness of sins and the penalty of adultery increase in the blessed days?

A: Yes, in blessed days and places, penalties are augmented according to the virtues of the time and place.

*   *   *

The penalty of defaming people
When a man and his divorced wife defame his present wife and accuse her of adultery, is their claim accepted? Is the dowry of the present wife canceled?

Q: A man married a righteous woman after he had divorced his former wife. He stipulated that if he had returned to his former wife, the dowry of his present wife would be paid immediately. Later, he returned to his former wife, and they defamed his present wife accusing

269

her of adultery and that she was pregnant out of adultery. Later, he divorced this second wife. What should be done by both? Is their claim accepted? Is her dowry canceled?

A: All praise be to Allah, the Lord of the Worlds. As for the first divorced wife and the man, they are to be lashed eighty whips if the accused woman demanded for implementing such penalty. Once lashed, their testimony will never be accepted because they are deviant.

Can he escape such penalty by having recourse to Li`an? There are three opinions in Ahmed's juristic school. Some say that he can have recourse to Li`an, others say he can not while still others say that he can do so if there is a baby which he wants to deny as his son. Even in case of Li`an, she deserves her dowry as mentioned by the Prophet (peace be upon him). This ruling is delivered according to the unanimous agreement of Muslim scholars.

Yet, as mentioned above, there are three opinions as far as Li`an is concerned:
1. The man is not to make Li`an. Instead he is to be lashed eighty whips because of accusing his wife of adultery. Besides, his testimony will never be accepted. This is one of the opinions of Imam Ahmed and Shafi`i.
2. The man is to make Li`an according to Abu Hanifah and Ahmed in another narration.
3. If the woman is pregnant, he should have recourse to Li`an just to deny that the baby belongs to him.

Otherwise, he is not to make Li`an. This is the other opinion of Ahmed and Shafi`i.

* * *

Having hashish
Is it prohibited to have hashish?

Q: What is the legal judgment on having hashish?

A: Hashish is a damned thing. Whoever has it or believes it to be permissible is damned. It incurs the wrath of Allah, His Messenger and the righteous believers. Whoever has it is exposed to the punishment of Allah. Hashish reduces one's enthusiasm and jealousy over his female relatives and spoils one's mood. There are many detrimental sides in having it and this makes it prohibited. Allah knows best.

* * *

Masturbation
Is masturbation prohibited for men and women alike?

Q: Is masturbation prohibited for men and women alike?

A: According to the majority of Muslim scholars, it is prohibited. Whoever does it is to be punished someway or other. Yet its penalty is not like adultery. Allah knows best.